THE L

COLBY JUNIOR COLLEGE

to Alexandra Township

ROBERTS AVE.

JULES ST.

MAIN REEF RD.

RUSTENBURG RD.

CITY LIMITS

JOHANNESBURG

Palacios

Naught for Your Comfort

TREVOR HUDDLESTON, C.R.

Doubleday & Company, Inc.
Garden City, New York
1956

Library of Congress Catalog Card Number 56–8495

Copyright 1956 by Ernest Urban Trevor Huddleston
All Rights Reserved
Printed in the United States at
The Country Life Press, Garden City, N.Y.

To
NORMAN MONTJANE
and the Africa he represents
this book is dedicated
with deep gratitude and love in Christ

PREFACE

THIS BOOK has been written in the odd hours of an exceedingly busy year. Perhaps that fact alone may give it value, for it has certainly come red hot out of the crucible which is South Africa today.

Many books about the Union of South Africa have appeared of recent months, and many more yet to come, for it is a country of inexhaustible fascination and interest. This book can claim only to throw light upon one small corner of the country, and it springs from a personal experience which is limited and confessedly partial.

Yet I have been a South African citizen: and I freely chose my citizenship. I wished to live and die a South African citizen, though I would have preferred with Alan Paton, to be called a citizen of Africa: an African, in fact. I am also a Religious, that is to say, a member of a monastic Community of the Anglican Church. In our Rule we are bidden "to have all things common" and not to use the pronouns "I" and "Mine." I must ask the Community's forgiveness for doing so in this book. But I have done so for two reasons: first, for the obvious one of literary style; secondly, because the opinions expressed here are entirely my own responsibility. They do not in any way reflect the common mind of the Community, though I believe many of my brethren are in substantial agreement with them. Yet without the love and support of the Community I should

7

never have had the joy and splendour of these twelve years in South Africa, nor the strength to make any kind of use of them.

I must thank especially those people who have made this book possible: Miss Mary Whitnall and Mrs. R——— L——— for their labours in typing, and Robin Denniston of William Collins for his patience, pertinacity and encouragement. I would also thank Alan Paton and his wife for a week of kindness and hospitality which I shall always remember and which made the completion of this book a pleasure.

Finally, I would thank Anthony Sampson and Harry Bloom for giving me the nerve to write it at all.

TREVOR HUDDLESTON, C.R.

Johannesburg
September 1955

CONTENTS

NAUGHT FOR YOUR COMFORT

I tell you naught for your comfort,
Yea, naught for your desire,
Save that the sky grows darker yet
And the sea rises higher.

GILBERT KEITH CHESTERTON
Ballad of the White Horse

I. Out of Africa

Ex Africa semper aliquid novi
PLINY

It is told of Smuts that when he said farewell to any of his friends or distinguished visitors leaving South Africa he quoted in that high-pitched voice of his the lines of De la Mare:

> *Look thy last on all things lovely*
> *Every hour.*

I have no doubt that to Smuts the loveliness of South Africa was its natural beauty and grandeur; its wild flowers and grasses, about which he knew so much; the great emptiness of its skies above the silence of the veldt.

But, since I knew of my recall to England by the Community to which I belong, those words have haunted me; and this book, written from the heart of the Africa I love, would be incomplete if I did not somehow set it in the context of this sudden, unwanted, but inevitable departure: *"Partir, c'est mourir un peu"* . . . and I am in the process of dying; in the process, "every hour." The thing about such a death, the quality of it, is to heighten the loveliness of what one is leaving behind. Without sentimentality or any foolish regrets it is most necessary to try to evaluate one's feelings, to try to discover and to relate that strange but deeply real truth which so many have experienced—the witchery of Africa: the way it lays its hold upon your heart and will not let you go. There are many exiles from Africa whose heart is still there and always will be. Why should it be so? I shall soon be one of them, so I must know the answer.

When fifteen years ago I stood before the High Altar in our great and beautiful conventual church at Mirfield to make my vows, I knew what I was doing. I knew amongst other things that the vow of obedience, willingly and freely taken, would inevitably involve *not* the surrender of freedom (as is so often supposed) but the surrender of self-will. I knew that it would involve, someday, somewhere, the taking up or the laying down of a task entrusted to me by the Community, a task to be done not of myself alone, and therefore not dependent upon my own desires or wishes. I knew what I was doing. I was glad to do it. I am still glad, and thankful, to have done it. For it is that vow of obedience which alone gives a man the strength, when he most needs it, to die by parting from what he loves. Nothing else could have torn me away from Africa at this moment. And no other motive than a supernatural one could be sufficient or strong enough to make sense of such a parting. Indeed, I should feel I had failed lamentably in all that I have tried to do if the parting were without tears. For it would mean that the work had been without love. So I have no complaints, no regrets (except for my failures and my sins), only a great thankfulness for the twelve years that are over and for the marvellous enrichment they have meant in my life.

"Look thy last on all things lovely . . ." Most of my time in South Africa has been spent in Johannesburg and half of it in one of the slums of that city of gold. No one,

I think, could call Johannesburg a lovely place. It is too stark and too uncompromising, too lacking in any softness of light and shade, too overwhelmingly and blatantly the centre of the Witwatersrand to have much loveliness. But I have seen momentarily the golden sand of the mine dumps crossed by grey and purple shadows in the evening, transformed into a real beauty—a thing impossible to the slag heaps of industrial England. And I have come to love the rolling country of the high veldt round the city, stretching away to the Magaliesberg Mountains and giving to Johannesburg a setting which belongs to few cities in the world. Of the beauty of its rich homes and gardens I will not write, for I have never been able to see that beauty without remembering the corrugated-iron shacks and the muddy yards where our African people live. Indeed, I am certain that no natural beauty could ever so lay hold on *my* heart as to make me weep for leaving it. Others may be created differently; I have never been able to feel that nostalgia for *places*, however lovely. And, after all, Africa is a cruel place rather than a beautiful one. She lives by extremes. Her storms and her sunshine are both fierce. Life itself is precarious and has to find a foothold by struggling against that barren rock, those scorching winds, that arid, sandy soil.

Johannesburg itself, which is the place I know and love best, would be by most people regarded as lying outside the real Africa: a cosmopolitan, crowded city—much like those smaller cities of America, new and brash and hard. . . .

"Look thy last on all things lovely . . ." What does it mean, then, this real agony of parting? Why does it cost so much? What I am hoping to say in this book will give the answer, if I am at all capable of giving it.

Spiritual writers spend quite a lot of time talking about "detachment." The lives of the saints are full of instances of this virtue, which indeed is a vitally necessary one in the Christian life. But generally the impression that such writers give is of a negative and cold quality: a refusal to allow oneself to become "attached" for fear that in some way such attachment would mean a base disloyalty to Christ. No doubt there are souls who for their own protection must eschew all human affection if they are to cleave to God in purity of heart. I am not one of them. For me, detachment is only real if it involves loving; loving to the fullest extent of one's nature—but recognising at the same time that such love is set in the context of a supernatural love of God. Then, when the moment of surrender, of parting, comes, one has a worth-while offering to make: an offering which is the love and affection of all the years, for all those one has known; it has some meaning, like the precious ointment poured out on the feet of Christ. And it is costly too.

"All things lovely . . ." Old Miriam from her room in Sophiatown writing to say good-bye . . . "We will miss that patting hand which reminds us of a certain King who had people who did not seem to know the way home. That King left his royal seat and came to live as one of them for thirty years, and for three years he tried to show them the way home. When he was satisfied that they knew the way, he left them. . . . May Heaven bless you, and if you do not come back to South Africa again we will meet at Jesus' feet."

"All things lovely . . ." The hands of a great multitude of little children stretched out in trust to grasp my own, to tug at the skirts of my cassock. And their eyes. The end of an All-African concert in my honour, and Tod

Matchikiza so excited that his composition has gone well. The timid knock at my door and Jonas, whom I thought felt nervous of talking frankly to me, "Father, there's a great problem I want to speak to you about . . ." And the jazz band, putting on their new uniforms for the first time . . . And the Congress—meeting out in the open square, "Mayibuye-Afrika": vitality, life, the Africa of the future . . . And so much else. So very much else.

This is the end of a chapter. And I thank God I have had the opportunity of living through it. The least I can do is to try to obey His voice from the darkness of the years that lie ahead. And I am certain that "all shall be well, and all shall be well, and all manner of thing shall be well"—for the Africa I love, the Africa of my heart's desire.

There are many different ways in which it would be possible to assess the situation in South Africa.

What I will attempt to do is to use certain legislation, certain authoritative statements,[1] and certain movements to illustrate a single theme. But not in any abstract and theoretical way; rather, as they affect the lives of persons, as I know them from day-to-day experience, as I feel them in my own heart at this moment. What I shall try to avoid is that most common and persistent error in all such assessments—the attempt to be impartial. By this I mean that I shall write this book as a partisan, for I believe that Christians are committed in the field of human relationships to a partisan approach. I believe that because God became Man, therefore human nature in itself has a dignity and a value which is infinite. I believe that this conception nec-

[1] See Appendix.

essarily carries with it the idea that the state exists for the individual, not the individual for the state. Any doctrine based on racial or colour prejudice and enforced by the state is therefore an affront to human dignity and *ipso facto* an insult to God Himself. It is for this reason that I feel bound to oppose not only the policy of the present government of the Union of South Africa but the legislation which flows from this policy. I am not interested, therefore, in any by-products of legislation which in themselves may appear to be beneficial to the African. I believe that a very great deal of harm is done in South Africa by people of good will and even better intentions who bend over backwards in their efforts to interpret Nationalist legislation in a favourable light. It is always possible, I suppose, even in the most vicious enactments of the most vicious governments to see elements of potential good. But Wilberforce would never have succeeded in abolishing slavery if he had listened to the arguments of kindhearted but wrongheaded slave owners. No advance can be made against prejudice and fear unless these things are seen as irrational and brought out into the fierce light of day. There is no room for compromise or fence-sitting over a question such as racial ideology when it so dominates the thought of a whole country. South Africans are very fond of describing their multi-racial society as unique; as a problem which does not confront other nations; as a situation demanding sympathy and understanding from the rest of the world. Equally they are almost pathologically sensitive to criticism from outside, whether it is expressed by a committee of the United Nations or by Canon Collins. Invariably the defence is that none can understand South Africa's problems except white South Africans. No one, apparently, can understand "the native" except his boss or his "missus." And none should dare to bring to the bar of world opinion (or of the Christian conscience outside the Union) such complicated problems. To do so is to be a traitor to one's country, an *uitlander* who refuses to recognise its claim to loyalty—in any case, a person whose opinions are valueless and can be ignored.

The truth is that the overwhelming majority of South Africans of the "white" group have no conception whatever of human relationships except that based on racial domination. The only Africans they know, they know as servants or as employees. Whilst the centre of the South African scene has shifted inevitably to the cities and their industrial areas, the vast majority of "Europeans" have no knowledge whatever of the urban African and his background. The greatest tragedy, in one sense, of the present situation is the total ignorance of those in responsible positions of government of the way in which young Africa thinks, talks, and lives. At least here, after twelve years of the closest possible contact with the urbanised African, I can claim an authority to speak at first hand. I would not dare to say that I can interpret the position perfectly, still less that I can prophesy when and in what form the inevitable revolt against present policies will come. That it *will* come I am entirely convinced. That there is no time to lose in breaking the present government I am also convinced. And, unlike many whose opinions I greatly respect, I believe that to do this the whole weight of world influence and world opinion should be brought to bear. If this is disloyalty to South Africa, then I am disloyal. I prefer to believe, however, that Christians are called to a higher obedience, a more profound patriotism than that due to a *de facto* government. The South Africa I love, the land to which I give all the loyalty that can be demanded, is

that which is built on a surer and more permanent foundation than white supremacy. It is the land which, at present,
exists only in the hopes, perhaps only in the dreams, of a
few: a land whose motto is even now emblazoned on the
Union coat of arms—*Ex unitate vires*—but whose behaviour and attitude are expressed in a real unity of races
and in a real strength of moral principle.

II. The Daylight and the Dark

Where the splendour of the daylight grows drearier than the dark . . .

G. K. CHESTERTON, *"The Aristocrat"*

IT WAS Holy Saturday in Sophiatown, the busiest day in the year for any priest who has charge of a parish as lively as that of Christ the King. For in order that Easter and the Lord's Resurrection shall be the most glorious and triumphant day in the calendar, there is much to be done in preparation. There are many confessions to be heard; there is the ceremonial of the New Fire to rehearse; there is the church to be made ready. And of course, as always in Sophiatown, there is a steady stream of people coming to the door to pay their church tickets or to ask one of the fathers to come and baptise a sick baby or to complain that the water has been cut off by their landlord and the drains are blocked. . . . So on this Saturday morning I was not too pleased when there strode into my office—and evidently angry—the young manager of the one and only milk bar in Sophiatown, an ex-serviceman who had begun a few months back an experiment—a European in an African township running an American-style soda fountain. "It's Jacob . . ." he began. "Father, I'm damn well going to do something about this. It's a bloody shame. . . . Father, you've got to help me. . . ."

On Maundy Thursday night at Jeppe station, Jacob Ledwaba had been arrested for being out after the curfew and without his pass. On Saturday morning he came home. He told his wife he had been kicked in the stomach in the cells and that he was in such pain that he couldn't go to work. Would she go and tell the boss and explain? It was this that brought the manager of the milk bar to my office at the mission on Holy Saturday morning.

It would be easy to dramatise this incident—and in many recent novels on South Africa such incidents have been described. All I want to say is this. Jacob was taken to hospital and died of a bladder injury, leaving a widow and a month-old baby. We brought a case against the police and in evidence produced affidavits concerning the nature of the injury from the two doctors who had attended Jacob. We also had the services of an eminent Q.C. The verdict (long after Jacob's body had been laid in the cemetery, long after any fresh medical evidence could possibly come to light) was that he had died of congenital syphilis. The magistrate added a rider to his verdict to the effect that the police had been shamefully misrepresented in this case and that there was no evidence whatever inculpating them.

So Jacob died, in the first place because he had forgotten to carry his pass. In the second because, Good Friday being a public holiday in South Africa, he had spent twenty-four hours in the police cells in Jeppe.

This thing happened quite a long time ago now, and I suppose that if Jacob's son is still alive he is just at the beginning of his school days. It will be only a few years more till the day when he, too, must carry a pass. I only hope and pray he will not be so careless as his father was and forget it one evening when he goes to visit his friends. It can be very costly to forget your pass.

Now the impact of such an incident as this upon a priest is rather different, I suppose, from its impact upon the ordinary South African citizen. For to a priest, Jacob is Jacob Ledwaba, husband and head of a family; Jacob Ledwaba, member of the congregation at Christ the King; Jacob Ledwaba, whose babe I have baptised, upon whose lips I have placed, Sunday by Sunday, the Body of Christ, whose joys and sorrows I have known, whose sins—by the authority committed unto me—I have forgiven as he knelt beside me of a Saturday evening after evensong in the lovely church. To the ordinary South African citizen he is a native boy (and he would still be a boy if he lived to seventy) who hadn't got a pass and who was probably cheeky to the police when they arrested him. A pity he died. But we must have *control.*

I read again that the Archbishop of Cape Town wrote recently in some church magazine: "The extreme complacency of the publications of the State Information Office so far as I have seen them gives the impression that the Union of South Africa is a kind of earthly paradise for its inhabitants of every group. The accounts given by some of the visitors to this country suggest that the Union of South Africa is a hell on earth. The facts stated on both sides are mainly correct. But . . . the difference lies in the way in which the material is selected."

I wonder if it is really as simple as all that. I believe it to be not a matter of the way material is selected so much as the way in which one assesses the real meaning and purpose of life. On this level, hell is not a bad description of South Africa, nor a very great exaggeration. For, as I understand it theologically, the real pain and agony (expressed symbolically but very definitely by Christ in the Gospels) of hell is frustration. Its atmosphere is dread. Its horror is its eternity. When you are in hell you see the good but you can never reach it, you know that you are made for God but between yourself and Him "there is a great gulf fixed." It is not a bad description of the ultimate meaning of *apartheid*. And I am not at all sure that it is very far from the ideal which the present government of South Africa has set itself to actualise.

At least the frustration and the fear are the most obvious characteristics of the present time for the African. And there is a sense in which it would seem that they must remain so for a very long while. And of these elements of fear and frustration the pass laws are a peculiarly powerful instrument.

There is, some twelve miles from the centre of Johannesburg but lying very close to its northern suburbs, a place called Alexandra Township. It is one of those places which figure in Alan Paton's *Cry, the Beloved Country*, whose atmosphere he has evoked so clearly that it would be impertinent for me to try to add to his description. It is, as it happens, the only African township of any size which lies to the north of the city. The great mass of Orlando, Moroka, Jabavu—where some quarter of a million Africans live—spreads westwards and continues to spread. But Alexandra Township, with its eighty to ninety thousand people, is a unique place. To begin with, it is not within the municipal boundary; then, it has a past history which has left it with certain freehold rights (a privilege exceedingly rare in the Union)—and it is quite desperately overcrowded. But its residents are part of the labour force of Johannesburg. They come in by bus and bicycle every morning to work in the homes, in the shops, and in the factories of the city. The long queue at the bus rank near the station of an evening does not disperse before 7 P.M. on any day of the week except Saturday. Without the Alexandra "natives" the northern suburbs would have to go servantless, and not a few commercial concerns in the city would be hard put to it to find labour. Apart from overcrowding (which is not restricted to Alexandra Township), there has been no major problem at Alexandra since the famous bus strike of some ten years ago, when, sooner than pay increased fares, the workers walked into the city to their work day after day until victory was won.

Now, however, there is a crisis—and one which has within it the seeds of a great tragedy. Only, like so many other crises in our country, it is unknown to most white citizens of Johannesburg and, though known, it is discounted by those in authority. The fact that it affects human life is of little account, for human life is as cheap as human labour if it is black, and as easily replaceable.

Those whose servants come day by day from Alexandra know it simply by name—as indeed do those whose servants come from Sophiatown and Orlando and Pimville. It is exceedingly rare for any European housewife to go and see the home of her wash-girl or her cook. Such concern is not normally included in the kindness which is her boast, certainly not included in the knowledge of natives which is her constant defence against criticism.

And so it comes about that in Alexandra an entirely new and major social problem has arisen, of which Johannesburg is unaware—but which affects the lives of everyone in Johannesburg directly or indirectly all the time.

The problem is this. Because of a new regulation concerning the influx of African labour into the city, no African who was not born in Johannesburg—no African, rather, who cannot prove that he was born there—is entitled to seek or to find work in the city. Those who are already in employment may continue to be so employed (with the exception of domestic servants who wish to change their jobs—I will say more of them later); but none may come into the city with the purpose of working unless he can prove birth and domicile. Now Alexandra Township is *not* Johannesburg. Although it exists and has always existed to serve Johannesburg; although its householders, its tenants, its sub-tenants are the labour force of the city; and although the only reason why they live in Alexandra is because of its proximity—it is not Johannesburg. Strangely enough, it only becomes interesting to the City Council and citizens of that immensely rich and comfortable place when, in dreams of further expansion northward, it is felt to be a barrier, a "black spot," a menace. Then it has significance. Today—because of this new regulation and the fierceness with which it is being enforced, hundreds of youngsters who have been born there are being turned into gangsters and labelled *tsotsis*. The boys of Alexandra are rotting away in the overcrowded yards, in the dusty streets, at the corners, and on the alleys—*because they cannot get out to work even if they want to.* Absalom's father is working at the O.K. Bazaars. He has been there for fifteen years and more, and in the course of that time he has managed to buy his own property in the township. He has a large family, and Absalom is the oldest boy and has just left school. He isn't very clever. And in any case, with five more children to educate, there's no hope for him of a boarding school where he might be able to train for teaching. The only course open to him is a job in town— a job which will bring in just enough extra cash to clothe and feed the youngest children; just enough, too, to make it unnecessary for his mother to take in washing and strain herself in the last months of her latest pregnancy. A job! To be able to join the early-morning queue at the bus stop with his father; to be able to feel that at last he is a man —and that his manhood is worth something. To be able at the week's end to have some money in his pocket which hasn't been marked with the sweat of someone else's labour but his own, which hasn't been picked up from the dusty street where the dice fall. A job! And the satisfaction of a discipline through the day and of a relaxing and a resting when work is over. A job! And the companionship it brings with it—so different from that ganging up which he sees around him and which he fears because of its hidden vicious strength and pull.

But unfortunately Absalom has been born in Alexandra Township in his father's house. It is his home. And because it is his home, he must not dare to cross the boundary into the city to seek that job. He is a prohibited immigrant as surely and as completely as any other "foreign native" from Portuguese East or Nyasaland or the Federation. He is sixteen and able-bodied. He has had as much education in a mission school as most of the European boys who earn thirty pounds a month and more in the semi-skilled jobs in Johannesburg. But his world is narrowed to the place where he was born—the dust and the crowds and the squalor of the township—or, as the only alternatives, the kitchen or the garden of a European house, itself outside the municipal boundary, the labourers' quarters of any farmer anywhere in the Union of South Africa. Absalom does not usually choose, for his future, the kitchen or the stable. Young men have visions. Life, at sixteen, must offer something a bit more attractive than wiping dishes, scrub-

bing floors, cleaning cowsheds, planting potatoes. . . .
Even young Africans are young men; even young Africans
have their ambitions, their dreams, their promised land.
And these things must not be shadowed always by the
knowledge that they are unattainable.

So—for Absalom—even Alexandra Township offers a future preferable to that of the kitchen or the farm. Perhaps
it should not—but it does. And if he cannot get the money
and the freedom which Johannesburg alone can give, he
must get these things somehow where he is. He must get
them with the boys in narrow trousers who loaf their lives
away by old Kumalo's store. He must become a *tsotsi,* a
cosh-boy, a wide-guy—because at least there's excitement
that way, while it lasts. He is a prisoner already. He is
outside the law as soon as he sets foot in the city. He can
feel himself a pariah—because he wants work when he cannot get it. He will, after all, join Joel and Zaccy and Punch
and the rest and see how he makes out. It is not long before he has a revolver of his own, money in his pocket,
and a hardness about him which even God's own grace
and power can barely smash.

An exaggeration? Most people would say so who live
in the pleasant places of the richest city in Africa: in those
wide-spreading suburbs of Johannesburg which make it
an earthly paradise. But then, most people in Johannesburg think Alexandra Township is next door to Sophiatown. Most people in Johannesburg prefer not to think of
it at all. And as for Absalom—he is a "skellum," a *tsotsi*
—"the kind of kaffir who ought to be sjambokked every
day; it would teach him sense." It would also teach him
not to indulge in the golden dreams of youth when you
live in Alexandra and haven't a pass.

I suppose that anyone who has lived in Sophiatown—

or one of the "Native Urban Areas" of South Africa—could write a book about the pass laws and nothing else. It would be a very terrible book, but it would not cause the slightest ripple of disturbance in South Africa. And of course there are not so very many Europeans who have had the privilege of living in Sophiatown. No. It is not so much the hatreds, the fears, the brutalities which are the basic social evils of our country—it is the ignorance and, with it, the acceptance of the evil.

So I could tell you the story of Jonas—of Jonas who was home from school for his summer holidays and who was arrested one morning and charged with being a vagrant. When I heard about it, it was already late afternoon, and by the time I had reached the police station he was waiting in the yard before being locked up for the night.

"Where was your school pass?" I asked him.

"They tore it up."

Luckily the wastepaper basket was still there; luckily I found the pass—in four pieces. And when I refused to surrender it to the sergeant in the charge office I was arrested myself. But at least I had the satisfaction, a few days later, of a complete apology, cap in hand (and not metaphorically either) of the commandant, who later became Commissioner of the South African Police. Yet for every boy like Jonas whose arrest was reported to me, there are a thousand who have no one to care, a thousand for whom a torn-up pass might mean ten days in prison, the loss of a job, the beginning of that swift and terrible journey into crime. For another consequence of the pass laws—a consequence known to every intelligent South African at all interested in penal reform—is that it leads to an absolute contempt for the law. If it is a crime to be in the street without a pass, without a bit of paper in your pocket, and if that crime is punished automatically with a fine that you cannot pay or a sentence of imprisonment—well, why not commit a crime that is worth while? You stand as good a chance of getting away with it as the next man. You stand the chance, too, of making something for yourself. The magistrates' courts, every day of the week, are crowded with pass offenders. Even if, as is generally the case, the magistrate is a just man and an honest, he has no alternative but to administer the law as if he were in care of a turnstile at a football ground.

"Charge?"

"Section 17—vagrancy."

"Guilty or not guilty?"

The prisoner looks bewildered; the interpreter impatiently snaps out the words again in Xosa or Zulu or Tswana.

"Not guilty," and a fumbling attempt to explain why his pass is out of order; a brief intervention by the official who attends the court on behalf of the pass-office authorities.

"Thirty shillings or ten days."

The prisoner is bundled down the steps to the cells, and another takes his place. His case has taken two minutes. If he is fortunate a friend will pay his fine. If not, he will remain in prison till his sentence, and very probably his job, is finished. And so a vast force of able-bodied men is, in fact, compulsorily confined in a building supported to house half the number; men who, for the most part, are simply technical offenders but who are in South Africa criminals.

In spite of a most excellent and, incidentally, expensive Commission on Penal Reform, whose report included the most damning exposure of the dangers to society inherent in the system I have described, the system still goes on. The report of the Commission was tabled in the House of Assembly over five years ago, but nothing so constructive as penal reform can find a place on the agenda—particularly when it concerns the effects of the pass laws on crime. It is not crime that matters, it is control. And to have that control, to know that any native can be stopped in the street and questioned, can be turned out of bed at night or in the early hours of the morning, can be arrested first and questioned afterwards—to have that control, why that is proof of supremacy: that is *baasskap,* that is our solution of the racial problem. At least it is part of our solution. The only serious defect in the system is that the real criminal always has a pass—he can buy one for fifteen pounds any day of the week, and it is well worth the money.

But all these things have been said, have been written about, have been part of every discussion on racial problems for the past twenty years and more. And even though it may happen only once in a while, every European citizen of Johannesburg experiences sooner or later the arrest of his houseboy or the disappearance of his cook. It is part of the pattern of life. And on the whole it is a pattern which is wonderfully acceptable—for it carries within it the great idea, of course: of power, of supremacy for whiteness. It is so comforting, too, to the conscience to be able to go and pay the fine or sign the admission of guilt and bring Jim back again to his job in the kitchen. It must (surely it must) fill his heart with gratitude to the missus or the *baas,* to know that they will take that trouble, to know that they really want to be just. ("But I must remember to deduct thirty shillings from his wages this month to cover the fine.")

Every citizen experiences it. But every African boy lives in the shadow of it from the moment he leaves the classroom behind him for the last time. And it does not matter, either, what position in society he reaches. He is never beyond its grasp. It is indeed the shadow—his own black shadow—that is with him always. So a young African priest, a member of my own Community just back from his ordination in England and wearing the habit of his order, was arrested and handcuffed at nine o'clock one morning and brought to me at the priory because he had no pass. The European policeman who brought him was a tall, callow, gawky youth who stood in front of me, hands on hips, cigarette drooping wet from the corner of his lips. And when I was angry and turned him off the premises he said: "I'll arrest every bloody kaffir in this place if they break the law. . . ." And when that afternoon I went to report the incident to the commandant he was furious that the story had already appeared in the afternoon edition of the *Star*. But I have long learned that my only weapon in such cases is publicity, and so I explained to him. I was not surprised at his anger either, for I had expected it. But I was surprised when, after a few minutes of fierce rebuke (we were alone in his office), the commandant suddenly said, gently and wearily: "As a matter of fact, Father, you are quite right. If I could leave the force tomorrow I would. But it's my livelihood and my profession. So what can I do?"

A report on the Union's crime was recently published in one of the Johannesburg papers. This showed that, in one year, of 72,000 Africans convicted, more than 45,000 fell within the category of pass-law offenders. It showed further that a fifth of the time spent by the police on criminal proceedings of one kind or another was spent simply on pass-law offences. It revealed—what all of us who have had anything to do with the situation guessed already—that over half the time spent in the magistrates' courts was spent in dealing with crimes of this sort. "Pass-law crimes," said Brigadier Coetzee of Pretoria Police Headquarters, "are the only type of statutory offence which requires no docket to be opened, no witnesses to be questioned, and no statements to be taken. Non-production of a pass or a pass out of order is generally proof in itself that an offence has been committed. . . ." The proof and the offence are in fact identical: for if you are an African and you have left your papers at home you have committed a crime; you can be arrested and imprisoned immediately, and the quickest and safest way to get your release is to pay an "admission of guilt" fine without argument. The fact that you are not guilty of any real offence is beside the point. You are an offender because, by accident, you have tried to evade the control of the state. You have walked freely where you would and have shared the sun-bright air with your neighbour; or perhaps you have actually stood in a bus queue in order to reach your home; or perhaps you have gone to post a letter or to buy a soft drink. . . . But without a pass you are not entitled to such liberties, and it is the duty of the police to remind you of the fact, for only in this way is control possible.

One of the terrible things that happens after a while to all of us in South Africa is the acceptance, unwilling or otherwise, of a situation which cannot be justified on any moral principle but which is so universal, so much a part of the whole way of life, that the struggle against it seems too great an effort. And this attitude affects the African as much as the European. For so long have passes been woven into existence itself, for so long has it been the right

33

and the duty of every policeman to stop, to search, and to question anyone, anywhere, at any time, that the resistance and the will to resist have almost died. And I am as guilty in this respect as anyone else. For, although I get angry when the boys in my school are arrested on their way to the shops (and what schoolmaster in any country would need to spend hours of his time issuing and collecting passes?), I pay their "admission of guilt." I become part of the system. I accept it. Even, sometimes, I get exasperated when one of my own employees fails to produce the necessary papers—exasperated because it will mean for me, as well as for him, hours of wasted and profitless effort. It is easier to obey, easier to be guilty of connivance at an evil, easier, even, to say to oneself, "Well, perhaps it's not so bad after all. It's the law. They're used to it. Why worry?"

Why worry? If the instances I have quoted were just isolated moments, the kind of thing that happens in any society through the failure of the individual, or the weakness of that human nature which is the basis of society, perhaps there would be no need to worry. At least the Christian in this world is warned often enough to regard himself as a "stranger and pilgrim . . . with no continuing city." And the priest—if he is even feebly aware of his purpose and function—knows well enough that man is a frail and wayward creature.

Unfortunately it is not the isolated cases of cruelty, of sordid motive, or of plain stupidity which make the indictment of the pass laws so grave a matter. It is the whole foundation upon which they, like the policy of *apartheid* itself, rest. For, basically, the underlying assumption of the pass laws is just this—that discrimination is justifiable and even commendable if it ensures the permanent superiority of one race over another; if it ensures control, *baasskap,* domination.

And from this assumption, or perhaps as the origin of it, there flows that other even more deadly thing—the depersonalisation of man. This most characteristic modern phenomenon—the submerging of the individual in the mass —is nowhere more manifest than in South Africa today. And it is nowhere more clearly or more devastatingly exampled than in the operation of the pass laws. A man is a native. A native must carry a pass. A pass is his title to existence, his guarantee (so slender and so precious) of temporary freedom, his only excuse to authority for being where he is and doing what he does. In other words, man is reduced, because he is black, to an integer, a fingerprint in a file, a thing rather than a person. But a sentient thing, threatened and fearful because of the shape of the society of which he is a part.

I pray God I may never forget or weary in fighting against it, for it seems to me that as a Christian, and above all as a priest, my manward task is always and everywhere the same: to recognise in my brother more than my brother, more even than the personality and the manhood that are his; my task is to recognise Christ Himself. And I cannot, therefore, stand aside when it is He whom men treat contemptuously in the streets of the city.

"I was in prison, and ye visited me not. . . ."

III. Till There Be No Place

Woe unto them that join house to house, that lay field to field, till there be no place.

ISAIAH

I REMEMBER returning one evening from a day of committees and discussions to the mission in Sophiatown to find on the *stoep* a party of six men waiting patiently for my arrival. This was a familiar enough sight and one which, very often, I fear, I found daunting. It meant, always, a problem. And problems at the end of a heavy day and before supper and with other business to attend to—well, priests are only too conscious of their fallen human nature at such moments. But it was a winter evening, and winter in Johannesburg at six thousand feet with the wind blowing the sand in fine, icy blasts from the mine dumps is cheerless, to say the least of it. I did not know these men. They sat there on a bench, a silent group, waiting to tell me something that had brought them together. I asked them in. Their story was a simple one and very simply told. They lived in one of the yards in Edith Street, just a couple of blocks away from the mission house. Like thousands of other Johannesburg Africans, their home was a row of corrugated-iron shacks built in the very restricted area behind someone else's house. Each man had his family in one room and paid the landlord perhaps thirty shil-

37

lings a month rent for it. It was not much of a home: hot
in summer when the sun struck down on the iron roof and
there was no ceiling to protect you, cold in winter because
the wind penetrated the joints and angles and there were
no walls save the iron itself. But it was a home, nevertheless. It was twelve square feet of room that you could call
your own for the time being, a place to come back to at
the end of the day, a place to lie down in.

This morning the men had gone to work as usual, leaving their wives and children still asleep under the blankets.
They had returned in the dark evening to find the roofs
stripped from their shacks, their families squatting in the
open round a brazier, their children crying with cold and
the desire for sleep. That was the reason for their visit to
me. And their question—such a familiar one in Sophiatown
and in all the days and years that I have lived in African
Johannesburg—"Father, what can we do?"

I went with them to see for myself, and I found a
woman in labour amongst those round the brazier, and
her baby was born under the winter stars that night.
"There was no room for them at the inn"—and so, on a
winter night in Bethlehem nearly two thousand years ago,
the Son of God had entered His world in the bleak and
barren shelter of the stable. It has come back to me again
and again in the richest city of the Southern Hemisphere
just how easily man can reject the Christ he proclaims to
worship. But in that dejected little group in Edith Street
the picture of Bethlehem and the rejection there came to
life. It has never left me and I pray it never will. I think
that the carols of our day, beautiful as they are, can dis-
tort the truth; can be a dangerous escape from the realities
of the Christian faith if we do not remember that, in fact,
God's entry into the world was unwelcomed and uncared

for when it happened; that "He came unto His own and His own received Him not." Perhaps I am reading back into the event thoughts which did not so crowd in upon me at the time—it is over five years ago now. But that sight, I am sure, made me more determined to try to arouse the public conscience on the issue of African housing than anything else. It also made me risk an action for contempt of court.

When the whole story was told me it went something like this. There are in Johannesburg today some forty thousand African families with no homes of their own. These are the labour force of the city, the people upon whose work it utterly depends. Five years ago there were slightly more, and houses were being built so slowly that they had no hope of owning one. So in Sophiatown and Alexandra Township and on the peri-urban fringe, shacks were built in back yards of existing houses. It increased the density of population to danger point. There was a risk from the public health angle. There was the creation of a slum within the meaning of the act. The landlords who had allowed their property to be used for this purpose were warned by the local authority that such shacks must be destroyed within a certain short period. Otherwise they themselves would be prosecuted. They were in a dilemma. Either they had to turn whole families on to the street, or they had to risk prosecution and punishment. "Father, what can we do?" Finally, without warning, the authorities themselves took action and chose a winter day on which to do it. That was why those six men, returning tired and hungry from the city, found their homes destroyed and their families under the stars and the wind blowing the sand and the dust of the street about them. "Father, what can we do?" What indeed? It would not be at all difficult, in the English context of such a situation, to give the answer. The power of the vote, the fact of representation at a local level, the influence of the press—these things are generally sufficient to make protests worth while. It is not so in South Africa, for the Africans. Indeed, although Sophiatown is a rate-paying suburb, highly assessed for the purpose, there has never been any way by which the City Council could be made to take an interest in it. There has never been any form of representation for its residents at any level. And in the whole long history of its development over the past fifty years the "improvements" of made-up roads, water, sewerage, and electric light have had to be fought for and won by interested Europeans, often against a dead weight of official inertia and lethargy. It is not so very long ago, after all, that if you wanted water in Sophiatown you had to walk three or four miles to the nearest white suburb and carry it back on your head. You paid a penny a bucket for clean water and a halfpenny for dirty —and in that water quite a lot of the laundering of European Johannesburg was done.

"Father, what can we do?" I persuaded one of those landlords, George Ndhlovu, who had received an eviction order for his tenants, to allow himself to be brought to court, and I promised that I would be there on the day. In the meanwhile I asked Dr. Ellen Hellmann (now president of the South African Institute of Race Relations), who perhaps knows more than any living person about the social and economic structure of urban Africa, to accompany me on a deputation to the authorities. It was, at the time, an interesting experiment. I have since learned to anticipate the kind of reception we met with that day. It is no longer interesting—merely inexpressibly exhausting.

We went first to the Medical Officer of Health. In his

office he sat at a broad desk playing with paper clips. When I had explained my business he rang a bell for one of his inspectors. "You see, Father, this is the position. . . . Hundreds of these tin shacks, most insanitary because there are not sufficient latrines for this surplus population. . . . Danger is acute from the public health side, and I have to administer the law. . . . All these people have been warned not to allow shacks on their property. . . . They go on building. . . . Mr. Smit here" (he turned to the inspector) "will give you the figures for one street. . . ."

I tried to explain that I was only too familiar with the facts. I didn't want any figures. Those stinking yards I had visited a hundred times; into those shacks I had only this morning carried the Body of Christ. "I wholly agree," I said, "that the slum conditions are there. No one is so foolish as to deny it. But the reason is also as plain as a pikestaff—there simply are not any houses available for the sub-tenants. With a waiting list of ten or fifteen thousand, where are these people to go? Will you tell me how to answer them when they come and sit on my *stoep* and ask me? Where are they to go?"

I remember his answer now, six years later, as clearly as if I had heard it for the first time. "That's nothing to do with me. My job is to administer the law as it stands."

"But you *can't* deal with people as if they were things; you can't turn them out on the street in winter without making any provision for them."

"I tell you, it's nothing to do with me. Go and complain to the Manager of Non-European Affairs; housing is his concern. Good morning."

So we went to the manager. He was a good man, perhaps the best the City Council has ever had. (It was not very long afterwards that he resigned in despair over the native housing policy of his department.) "Father, you know the situation. I've a waiting list here for houses in Orlando Township, and many of the people whose names are on the list have been waiting for ten years. This is a national problem. We simply cannot tackle it locally."

"Can't you, at any rate, urge the M.O.H. to hold his hand for a bit? To wait at least until there's some possibility of accommodating people before throwing them on to the street?"

"Sorry. My department can't interfere. There's nothing I can do."

When I got back to Sophiatown I phoned the mayor's secretary and asked for an appointment. But when I explained what I wanted to discuss the appointment was not granted. "It's a matter for committee. You can bring a deputation if you like. The mayor can do nothing in his personal capacity. . . ." And that was as far as I could get when on a morning soon afterwards I was sitting at the back of "M" Court awaiting the case of my landlord. I had taken the precaution of warning the press to send someone to report the whole affair. I had also interviewed the public prosecutor before the court began its business and had explained the whole matter to him. He seemed to take a reasonable view. Anyhow, I felt I could do no more. . . . "George Ndhlovu . . ." He stood in the dock and the charge was read out to him. He began to answer questions from the prosecutor. . . . "I could not turn them out on to the street. . . . Yes, they paid rent. . . . No, I did not answer the first summons. . . ." The magistrate turned to the public prosecutor: "Any comment?" "I suggest a sentence to pay a fine of . . ."

This was the moment I had been waiting for, but I did not like it at all. Ridiculous to feel so scared when all that was needed was a word or two. It was a physical effort to stand up, an effort to force my voice to normality, an effort to look straight at the magistrate. "May I say something, Your Worship?" The magistrate looked a little surprised, but he asked what I had to say. "Simply that it is unjust to penalise a man for an offence which is not his fault but the fault of society. . . ." I would not say now that those were my exact words, but they were what I tried to say.

"That is enough. You must sit down. This is a court and you have no right to speak. . . ."

"I am sorry but I must repeat what I have said. . . ."

A policeman moved across the well of the court to where I stood. I took a glance at my pressman, and he was getting it all down. I felt better. "I shall not sit down till I have said what I came here to say."

The magistrate in some confusion ordered the court to be cleared, left the bench himself, and left me wondering what would happen next. I filled in the next few minutes by chatting to those Africans who had come to witness the affair: my friends, my own parishioners, the flock—or part of it—over which I had received authority to guard and keep my watch. Was it really the function of a priest to defy a magistrate? The particular magistrate who was in court that morning evidently did not think so, for he had brought with him his chief, and I was called out to a discussion in the lobby.

"I am surprised at you, a minister of religion, creating a disturbance like this. I will not have my magistrates attacked in this way. I must warn you. . . ."

I asked the chief magistrate what else I could have done. The M.O.H., the manager, the mayor—I had tried each one. The public prosecutor had promised to do his best and had in fact asked for the maximum penalty to be imposed on Ndhlovu. "Is it really the function of the minister of religion to remain silent in face of injustice?" The chief magistrate told me that there were consitutional methods of going about such things and that, he repeated, he would not have his magistrates bullied. We left it at that.

The *Star* that evening carried a fairly full account of all that had happened. It was on that evening, too, that Alan Paton, who had been for many years a friend of mine, was to give a public reading from *Cry, the Beloved Country* in aid of the African Children's Feeding Scheme. There was something very encouraging about listening to Alan that night in the drawing room of the Grand National Hotel. *Cry, the Beloved Country,* with its deep perceptiveness of the root of the problem, revealing to white South Africa for the first time the truth about racialism in its effect on persons . . . that marvellous yet almost inexpressible warmth one feels at certain moments when one's own mind and another's are at one. Msimangu's bitter yet so profound utterance, "I have one great fear in my heart, that, when they are turned to loving we shall be turned to hating."

Is it not to prevent this ghastly end that some of us at least are sent to take a stand, even if it is the rather pathetic one of making a nuisance of oneself in a magistrate's court? I thought so that night, and I think so today. I would not dare to say that what I did had any great or permanent effect. But I do know that within a week representatives of the City Council visited Sophiatown (a rare event in itself) and that for quite a while there were no more eviction orders issued to the landlords. Indeed, when I went round to Edith Street a few days later, I found that the roofs were on again, the women were standing in their own doorways, gossiping, the children were playing in the dirt and dust of the yard, and the pots were boiling. The men would come home again. They would come home—if only for a while. I think it was worth the effort.

There is in this incident of George Ndhlovu nothing perhaps very startling, nothing very novel. Yet it has for me, within itself, certain fundamental principles of the Christian faith. And here in Johannesburg it is somehow easier to see those principles clearly and at the same time to realise how few people there are who seem to value them at all. It is the priest's task, or one of them, to stand in the pulpit Sunday by Sunday and to preach the moral law of the Church. It was Father Basil Jellicoe, that magnificent priest of the St. Pancras slums, who first inspired me with the thought—which has since become a passion—that it is a mockery of God to tell people to be honest and pure and good if you are making these things impossible by consenting to the evil of bad housing. "Consenting," in Johannesburg, is the operative word. I do not think that its citizens are any worse, any less compassionate, than those of London or New York. I have very good reasons for knowing how generous they can be if their hearts are touched —though the unpredictability of their generosity is also a strange thing. But they can go on living in a fantastically unreal world in spite of what they *know* to be true.

It has always, for instance, amused me to think that those who go and enjoy themselves at the Country Club—an expensive and very beautiful place by any standards—are doing so within a mile and a half of the "black spot" of Sophiatown. In all probability their "girl" or their "garden-boy" has a home there too. They know it as a name (who can fail to, who reads the press?)—but they have never been there, and they have no sense of obligation which would move them to go. So, day after day, those whose home is a shack in Newclare or a breeze-block shelter in Orlando or a mud-brick hovel in Moroka set off to work in one of the lovely suburbs of Johannesburg. They spend their time in the kitchen or the laundry, washing and cleaning, using every kind of American gadget, looking upon gleaming white walls and stainless-steel sinks and pretty furniture. Or perhaps, if male, they drive the boss to his office or to his factory in the Cadillac and spend the morning adding to its polish. Then they return in the over-crowded train to Newclare and Orlando and Moroka—to the shack and the shelter and the hopelessness of making it any different.

The point is this. In a South African city it is not merely the contrast between wealth and poverty which is so obvious. It is the fact that this contrast is *forced* upon the African every day of his life—for he lives in one world and his master in another, and he must move from one to the other all his days. It is the fact, too, that it is not merely a contrast between wealth and poverty that he sees—it is a contrast based upon the accident of colour. Wealth is white; poverty is black. Both co-exist in the same city within a few miles of one another. The contrast is compulsory, inevitable, and, for most Africans, unending. For the European it is never so. The native who works for him is either a "good boy" or a "skellum"—and, if the latter, he does not work for him for long: there are plenty of others. The "girl" in the kitchen (who is probably the mother of a family in spite of her name) is nowadays considered almost certainly "difficult" or "spoilt" or "ungrateful"—and is regarded as a potential thief from the moment she sets foot in the place of her labours. But she is still a necessity—as much so as the electric iron or the Aga stove

—part of one's way of life. European contact with Africans in the city is limited entirely to this master-servant relationship. Every judgment, every opinion as to the future of "the native question," is in fact based upon it. The real life of the African—his home, his family, his interests—is as unknown to the European in Johannesburg as it is to the European in Paris. And so it is that the colossal problem of housing has been left untouched for so many years. And with that problem all the other social problems, which are religious and ethical problems too, are inextricably mingled and are unknown to white South Africa.

The "crime list" is published daily in the newspaper and read with concern over the breakfast coffee in Parktown. The increase in crimes of violence, the general sense of insecurity which it brings, the thefts and the assaults and the alarming spread of juvenile delinquency—these things are read about every day, and with concern. But the background to the problems—the home and family life of the urban African—that is behind a barrier which must not be penetrated. Just occasionally the barrier is breached for a few hours or a few days through some external accident or catastrophe. Then white Johannesburg wakes up, sets about things in a frenzy of activity, satisfies its conscience —and sleeps.

Such an accident (called, euphemistically "an act of God") happened two or three years ago when a tornado struck Albertynville. Albertynville belongs to what is known as the "peri-urban area" of the city. That is to say it is outside the jurisdiction of Johannesburg City Council, and the Board which is its governing body has rather too many commitments to make its own jurisdiction very effective. It is about ten or twelve miles from the centre of the city—a squatters' camp sited on a particularly bleak and barren piece of veldt. The land is owned by an individual who charges rent to each squatter electing to build his shack there. Amenities are almost entirely lacking. It is just a conglomeration of lean-to, corrugated-iron, and mud-brick dwellings, with water, of a kind, not too far away. Albertynville is just one of many such camps on the perimeter of the city, and it houses several hundred of those who work there. It is no worse and no better than scores of other similar places. But on the night of the tornado it looked very much like a no man's land in Flanders in the 1914–18 war. The force of the wind had simply ripped roofs off and carried walls away as if they were made of paper (and some of them almost were anyway!). The rain had left sodden mounds of rubble where a few hours before men and women had prepared and eaten a Sunday dinner. Against a stormy and moon-bright sky the wreckage of the camp stretched out its strange and knotted fingers. But what was most striking about the whole, eerie scene was, in the first place, the absence of all Africans; in the second, the long line of shining motorcars which for hours had been streaming out of European Johannesburg to bring assistance. It was extremely difficult to get near the place unless you knew a side route. Ever since the wireless announcement two or three hours before, the public had been racing to the scene. But by ten o'clock that night (the tornado had struck in the early evening) there was no resident in sight. All had vanished into the neighbouring camps—or perhaps into the wide veldt itself. When the whole situation had been properly assessed it was discovered that between a hundred and two hundred families had been rendered temporarily homeless. But the sight of those forlorn bits of wreckage that had been "houses"—the old iron tins and biscuit boxes, the mud crumbling into slime, the timber from packing cases—struck at the heart of white Johannesburg. Money, clothes, provisions—a mayor's appeal to give the final stamp of authority to such a providing—came pouring in. For a week Albertynville and its inhabitants were the target for generosity in a big way. I have no doubt that those who were dispossessed of home and property by that tornado received compensation such as they had never dared to imagine. And the aftermath of it all, in white Johannesburg, was a faint and uneasy stirring of the mind. "Do our natives really live like that? Are those pictures true? Isn't it time something was done about native housing? After all, it must be dangerous from the health point of view, and disease knows no colour bar. . . ." But it was only a faint and uneasy stirring. Within a month it was forgotten. Albertynville is still there, and its inhabitants have returned to new disfiguring shacks upon the veldt.

The door, however, had been opened a little. It all helped us in our crusade (for such it became) to persuade the local authority and the government to do some building. The moral of the Albertynville story is, I suppose, a not unusual one anywhere. Man can live alongside of an evil all his life and refuse to recognise it, still less to think that it is his duty to do anything about it. Lazarus lay at the door of Dives for a very long while, and no doubt the rich man drove past him time and again as he left his home and returned of an evening. If he thought about him at all, he was conscious of a sort of resentment against the society which allowed beggars, rather than of his own duty to a fellow man. It took the shock of hell to awaken Dives. And then it was a bit too late to do him much good. I have sometimes thought that in the Dives and Lazarus society which is Johannesburg there is no shock which is sufficiently strong really to arouse the public conscience for longer than a week on any vital issue. A tornado does not happen very often. And even that does not leave more than a rapidly fading memory of momentary kindness behind it. The shacks are still there.

Since I came to Johannesburg twelve years ago, some of my most interesting, as well as frustrating, experiences have been connected with the city's vast housing problem. To understand this it is essential to realise one fundamental principle of government policy—a principle absolutely involved in the doctrines of *apartheid* and white supremacy: the twin pillars upon which all development in South Africa must rest. It is the principle of migratory labour. Here I am not attempting to discuss this principle as it affects the gold mines; that is another subject altogether. Let me try to state the position as simply and as clearly as I can, and as I think Dr. Verwoerd (Minister of Native Affairs) would himself express it. First, social separation between the white and the black races is essential if white civilisation is to be preserved. Second, the presence of the native in industry is essential if the economy of the country is to retain its balance. Third, industry is located in the towns. How, then, can the social separation be maintained? It is not enough to make certain of geographical separateness by the creation of native locations and townships. History has shown that those locations which were outside the city twenty years ago have now been encircled and are inside European areas today. It is not enough to make regulations and to enforce entry restrictions in urban areas, for such regulations and restrictions tend to lose their force when they apply to more than half the total population of a town. It is not enough, either, to apply a colour bar which will cut the native off from almost every source of "West-

50

ern" culture by depriving him of the possibility of enjoying music or art or theatre. He has his own. You have to make sure that the native in the urban areas is, and knows that he is, there on sufferance. That he has no permanence of any kind. That he is a migrant whose sole purpose is to provide labour in factory and office and home for the white-man-boss. "There is no room," says the Minister of Native Affairs, "for him in European society above the level of certain forms of labour." The whole conception, there-fore, of native housing in the cities must be governed by this most vital consideration. There must be no perma-nence about it. It must be possible, if not by a tornado then at least by an act of Parliament, to remove an African township as soon as it becomes at all probable that it is taking root. It must be impossible for any African, what-ever his social position, whatever his wealth, to own his home in the town so that he can regard it as permanently his possession and that of his children. Freehold rights, therefore, are a fundamental denial of the very basis of *apartheid* and intolerable as such. All housing schemes and all efforts to catch up on the appalling backlog in hous-ing in Johannesburg must have one fundamental quality: impermanence.

In a speech in the Senate in June 1955, Dr. Verwoerd gave official expression to the desirability of the migratory labour system, not only on the mines but in other direc-tions as well. "I believe," said the minister, "that the strengthening of this system and the extension of it to other fields of work for the natives will be in their interests, be-cause the vested business interests in the European towns would see that the urban locations never grew to be full-grown native towns. *Such a development also did not ac-cord with government policy.*" Dr. Verwoerd is generally logical. In the whole vast issue of native housing, his chief concern is to demonstrate that the native labourer is in the city for one reason only—the labour he can supply. So although Johannesburg is ringed round on its western circumference with the vast townships of Orlando, Moroka, Jabavu, and the rest; although these African locations have today something over a quarter of a million inhabitants— *there must be no permanence.* These are, in reality, labour camps, though often enough, in the better built areas, the houses are sufficiently strong to last for generations. The monotonous rows of "pre-fabs," so familiar in Europe, have been reproduced in Johannesburg.

There has been little imagination in the planning and none at all in the approach to a community-conscious town in a place such as Orlando. It is a "location"—a "place for natives"—that is the South African ideal: an abstraction which will serve its purpose and which will be conveniently forgotten. It is a "location" in another sense also—a "place" which today is and tomorrow can be elsewhere. That the people living in it should care where they live, or have a love for their homes, or dream dreams of having somewhere to spend their old age—that is a secondary consideration. In the eyes of Dr. Verwoerd it is not worth considering at all, for it is undesirable. The African is in the town to work. That is his function. If he desires a fuller life and a sense of "belonging," then he must go to the Reserves.

"The *apartheid* policy" he said, "is one of getting the natives to grow from their own roots out of their own institutions and from their own powers. It is a policy of gradual development, through mother tongue and own environment, to bring the natives to literacy and usefulness in their own circle." And so although there are today millions of Africans in the urban areas and, of those millions, hundreds of thousands who have been born and bred there, the town is not and must not be their home. Although their labour is the foundation of the whole South African economy and forces them into daily contact with the industrialised society of Western man, their future is in their past, in "their own circle," in the tribalism that the white man has done his best to smash to bits and that migratory labour destroys more swiftly than anything else could.

Together with so much else that is wrong or positively evil in South Africa today, the roots of the African housing problem go much deeper than the past seven or eight years of Nationalist rule. They flourish in the sort of apathy and selfishness which belongs to man himself but which seems to find a peculiarly strong expression in the wealthy city of Johannesburg. I remember a March day in 1944. I happened to be in Orlando that morning. Looking across at the main road which runs through the location, I saw a few little groups of people, women and children mostly, carrying or dragging along behind them a great bulk which was hard to distinguish. As they marched, what at first appeared to be a few became a growing but straggling rout of people. The bulky shapes upon their backs or in their hands or on their heads were in fact their household goods. In the late afternoon there were hundreds of people, hundreds of families streaming out on to the veldt, erecting shacks of mealie stalks, hessian, poles, biscuit tins, old iron —anything that would provide shelter. As the week wore on they were joined by hundreds more, some of whom had travelled from far along the Reef—to face a winter under such conditions rather than wait any longer for the houses that were never built.

So the first of Johannesburg's shanty towns came to be built—on municipal land, in protest against the seemingly endless delays to provide housing. It was called "Sofasonke"—which, being interpreted, means "we shall all die together." That was eleven years ago. Today, in the very centre of Orlando, there remains the evidence of that terrible time: it is called "The Shelters." It houses some thirty thousand Africans in lean-to, breeze-block sheds which were built as a temporary measure to house the squatters. The promise was that these shelters would be demolished within five years and their inhabitants housed decently elsewhere. But eleven years have passed. The population has grown by natural increase. Almost every shelter—in area roughly twelve feet by ten—has been the home of its original family through those long days. *Stoeps* have been added, doors fitted to the empty frames, windows built in. But the streets still stink with the effluent, there is no drainage, there is nothing which would encourage a man or a woman to live decently; indeed, there is no possibility of decency in those dark and fearfully overcrowded cells for which the City Council charges rent. So thirty thousand people who are the labour force of one of the richest cities in the Southern Hemisphere rot away in those long alleys and have nowhere else to go.

When winter set in in the first year it was essential to do something for the women and children. I remember especially well a certain Saturday afternoon when the wind was blowing dust across the veldt and the frail little shanties were almost torn from their moorings. The Council had decided to erect soup kitchens. The people had decided to boycott them. We had decided to open our mission school as a place of refuge for the women and children to sleep in that night. I went to see Mpanza, the leader of the squatters, and could not find him. Instead I suddenly heard the noise of men running and voices shouting. I was pulled from behind and shoved very hard into one of the shacks. "Quick, Father, stay in here; don't move till they've gone." I learnt that a gang of men, thinking I was in some way connected with the Council's soup kitchens, had run to attack me, and I had only just missed being hit with a knobkerrie from the rear. Not a very important incident, perhaps, but one which illustrates as well as any other the attitude of the squatters to the authority which offered them soup instead of homes. It is, unfortunately, the kind of offer which has been made a good many times in the past few years, as the shelters, standing grey and unsmiling on the bleak hillside, bear witness.

In January 1946, the same thing happened again. For months, through summer rains and winter winds, hundreds of families lived and hundreds of babies died in the shacks of "Tobruk." Father Michael Scott came and lived amongst the people and ministered to them as best he could. To my shame, I did very little to help him. Somehow it took me a long while to wake up, and it is good to be able to apologise publicly now for an apathy I cannot excuse. Eventually this second wave of squatters, and even a third, was moved to another "temporary" camp at Moroka—some twelve miles from the city and their work and on one of the bleakest bits of veldt imaginable.

Moroka Emergency Camp is now eight years old. It houses sixty thousand of Johannesburg's African citizens. Although the hessian has been replaced by tin or mud brick, and although deep pit-latrines have been provided, the "houses" are on plots twenty feet by twenty feet square. This is home. From it, in the dark dawn, the men go to work on bicycles or in crowded buses; to it they return, in the dark again when their day is done. This is home. It is impermanent. It is not even—yet—a location, though it soon will be when, please God, the shacks have been replaced with municipal houses.

In the meanwhile, eight miles nearer to the city on the same western circumference, men are pulling down with all the speed they can the houses of Sophiatown. For Sophiatown is that strange anomaly in South Africa, an urban area in which non-Europeans can actually own their houses and the land upon which those houses are built. Sophiatown has a quality about it—despite its overcrowding and its often squalid yards—which may not be allowed to exist in Dr. Verwoerd's country. It is, actually, a suburb! It is a suburb in the same way as Parktown or Westcliff or Waverley! It is, in fact, next door to two "white" areas. *And it has freehold tenure.* That is permanence. So it must cease to exist. But the story is quite a long one and needs a chapter to itself. In the meanwhile the Orlando shelters, the Moroka Emergency Camp, the fifty-year-old tin "tanks" which had been condemned as unfit for human habitation over twenty years ago—these places still stand. If cities fall under the judgment of God—as I believe St. John means us to understand from his apocalypse—then I have little doubt that Johannesburg will be condemned for this reason alone: that it accepted man's sweat and man's toil and denied him the possibility of a home. It is the stable of Bethlehem over again. "He came unto His own and His own received Him not."

IV. The Christian Dilemma

*If the trumpet give an uncertain sound, who shall
prepare himself for the battle?*

ST. PAUL

THE DUTCH REFORMED CHURCH took the initiative in December 1954 in calling a conference of Christian bodies to meet together to discuss the racial problems of South Africa. Not, of course, that this conference was the first to be held, but it was the first of its kind definitely sponsored by the church to which the majority of Afrikaners belong. The hall in which the meeting took place was "zoned," so that the white and black delegates should not sit together. One African minister, getting up to speak, prefaced his remarks by asking a question: "If Our Lord Jesus Christ came into this room this morning, on which side would He sit?"

That question is not a bad way of stating the dilemma in which Christians find themselves in South Africa. Rather an oversimplified statement of the problem, perhaps, but basically *the* problem all the same. And it is certainly not too soon for Christians the world over to know what is involved in it and why it is so vitally important to have some answer to it. In the first place, South Africa claims to be a Christian state. The present government gets more indignant in public over any challenge on this issue than previous governments. The leaders of the three "branches" of the Dutch Reformed Church have spent a great deal of time on debating whether *apartheid* is or is not consonant with biblical teaching and authority. The average citizen who attends church knows that somehow, by rationalisation or escape, he has to answer the same question posed by St. Paul in another context: "Is Christ divided?"

It is my considered opinion that unless the Christian Church in South Africa really faces this issue honestly within the next generation or less, it may well lose—and deservedly—the allegiance of the African people. And it is also my opinion, and one which is not only unpopular with those outside the Anglican Church but also with those in authority within it, that the issue is *not* being honestly faced nor properly presented to the conscience of the Christian world. After all, the Christian cannot escape the daily responsibility of choice, or if he does he is not in fact accepting the challenge of his faith. Yet in South Africa every day and almost every moment the white Christian is confronted with a choice of quite momentous consequence. The same choice, in fact, that was put before the priest and the Levite as they hurried past that torn and bleeding figure on the way down from Jerusalem to Jericho. The same choice that confronted Dives as he drove in and out of his mansion and hardly noticed the man lying at his gate, full of sores. The same choice, I would dare to say, that nearly tore the Christian Church asunder when St. Paul withstood St. Peter to the face over the admission of the Gentiles. "Who is my neighbour?" That is the question which Christians cannot evade; or if they do so in this life they must yet stand and answer one day before a more august Tribunal. "Who is my neighbour?" asked the clever young lawyer when he thought to destroy by mockery or argument the reputation of that upstart prophet from Nazareth. He got for an answer the parable of the good Samaritan. He was compelled to acknowledge, grudgingly but publicly, the possibility that racial difference and the prejudice that goes with it must submit to a higher law. Christians in South Africa are afraid even to ask the question. Can it be because deep in their hearts they know the answer and reject it?

The white Christian and the black profess the same allegiance to the same Lord. They recite the same Creeds, receive the same sacraments, have the same forms of worship. They use every day, no doubt, that prayer, common to all Christians, whose first words are: *"Our* Father . . ." But what of their relationship to one another in the city where they live out their lives? They can, it is true, pass one another in the street and so share the same air, the same shadows, the same blue sky. They can also meet together, master and servant, in a thousand different contexts: in kitchen, in factory, in office, in police court. This is contact. It is not relationship. It can never be love, αγαπη—the thing which Christianity is about. "Who is my neighbour?" He is the man I see entering the post office to post a letter—but he may not enter the same door as myself. "Who is my neighbour?" He is the man who makes my tea at ten o'clock and four and who brings it to me every day of my life in the office—but he cannot sit at table and drink it with me. "Who is my neighbour?" He is the child who comes to collect the washing on Mondays and to return it on Fridays, the child who passes a recreation ground with swings and seesaws and cool green grass but who may not enter it because it is labelled "European Children Only." Is this a sentimental approach to a problem which needs objectivity and a calm and reasoned solution? If it is, I cannot escape the charge of sentimentality. South Africa can do with a little more sentiment in these matters. It would be a refreshing change from the hypocrisy and rationalisation with which *apartheid* is justified from so many Christian pulpits and in so many Christian articles.

I was asked not very long ago to give an address to the group of African students in training at a government normal college near Pretoria. It was the students themselves who had asked me, and I took with me an African priest who acts as chaplain to the Anglican men in residence. My paper, as it happened, was an attempt to show the relevance of religion to the problems of everyday life: the kind of address which I imagine is given hundreds of times in English schools and colleges to young men who think that Christianity is outmoded and irrelevant. The principal of the college asked if he might attend: he was an Afrikaner and a member of the Dutch Reformed Church. At the end of the meeting he kindly asked me to have a cup of tea in his house. I told him I had an African priest with me. He thought hard for a moment, then invited both the priest and an African teacher to accompany us. As we walked across the veldt towards his house—set some distance from the college—he inquired with genuine surprise how I could believe that in fact Christianity had anything to do with such things as race relations, social problems, South African policies. Under a bright and unclouded moon I tried to answer, but I knew I was not understood. We reached his house. I was shown into the drawing room. The African priest and teacher were shown into the office. We all had tea—was it from the same pot?—and were treated courteously but separately. Only the light of the moon and the sounds of the veldt we shared as South Africans that night. I could, of course, multiply such an illustration many times. I have used it simply to show two of the characteristic features of the approach of the ordinary, good Dutch Reformed Christian to this question.

I would like now to consider that approach more carefully. But I would say at the outset that I am handicapped by a profound difficulty: that of not knowing personally more than one or two predikants—I can use only the official pronouncements of the churches concerned. Let me quote the most recent—that of the Commission for Current Problems of the Federated Ned. Geref. Kerke:

"Every nation and race will be able to perform the greatest service to God and the world if it keeps its own national attributes, received from God's own hand, pure with honour and gratitude. . . . God divided humanity into races, languages and nations. Differences are not only willed by God but are perpetuated by Him. Equality between natives, coloureds and Europeans includes a misappreciation of the fact that God, in His Providence, made people into different races and nations. . . . Far from the word of God encouraging equality, it is an established scriptural principle that in every community ordination there is a fixed relationship between authorities. . . . Those who are culturally and spiritually advanced have a mission to leadership and protection of the less advanced. . . . The natives must be led and formed towards independence so that eventually they will be equal to the Europeans, but each on their own territory and each serving God and their own fatherland."

It is only fair to say that this Commission's report was heavily criticised by several eminent Dutch Reformed predikants, including Dr. Ben Marais. Nevertheless, I believe it to be in general outline a completely just statement of an attitude and a theological view accepted by a very large number within that church and indeed outside it. It carries with it the implication that all racial differences are not only willed by God in His act of creation but are to be sustained by Him to the end of time. It further involves the assumption that there has been no intermingling of races through the centuries without loss and presumably sin—since such intermingling must be, *ipso facto,* contrary to the Divine Will. And it makes no mention whatever of the intervention of God in the world in the Person of His Son. In other words, the view here expressed (and I am convinced that, with some modifications and differences, it is the view of most Dutch Reformed Church members) *is sub-Christian.* I say sub-Christian rather than Old Testament because I suppose that somewhere behind the obscure and murky twilight theology it represents there are remembrances of the Gospel message. I cannot find them.

The truth is that the Calvinistic doctrines upon which the faith of the Afrikaner is nourished contain within themselves—like all heresies and deviations from Catholic truth—exaggerations so distorting and so powerful that it is very hard indeed to recognise the Christian faith they are supposed to enshrine. Here, in this fantastic notion of the immutability of race, is present in a different form the predestination idea: the concept of an elect people of God, characteristic above all else of John Calvin. And like so many other ideas transplanted from their European context, it has been, subconsciously perhaps but most really, narrowed still further to meet South African preconceptions and prejudices. It fits exactly the meaning which the Afrikaner likes to give to the Great Trek. Just as the children of Israel had their Exodus and their journeyings through the wilderness to the Promised Land—so the

Voortrekkers had to escape from the Egypt of British domination and to fight their way through against the on-
slaughts of the heathen. The place names on the map of
South Africa are a sufficient witness to the truth of what
I have written. Just as the children of Israel had a divine
mission, a divinely given leadership which set them apart
from and over against the indigenous peoples, the tribes
they had met with and conquered—so the "Afrikaner-volk"
also had its unique destiny on the continent of Africa. It
is to be for all time the nation representing purity of race:
whiteness, divinely ordained and given.

Logically, therefore, the native peoples also are part of
a divine plan. They are in South Africa by right also.
(Though it is a subject of debate whether they reached
the area now known by that name at the same time as or
before the white man.) But they must know their place.
They are to be led, to be guided, to be governed by the
chosen people. That is their destiny. It is written in the
Book. Or, if it isn't, it ought to be. Calvinism, with its great
insistence on "election," is the ideally suitable religious
doctrine for white South Africa. It provides at the same
moment a moral justification for white supremacy and an
actual day-to-day reason for asserting it. "Eventually they
will be equal to the Europeans . . ." but, thank God,
"eventually" will be when we are dead and our children's
children will have to face a new world in Africa. So we
must hope.

I do not think this is an exaggerated view of the underlying belief of the Dutch Reformed Church. And it is a
view not merely held and preached by the minister in the
pulpit. With all its faults and errors, the Dutch Reformed
Church seems to have succeeded, where many another
Christian body has failed, in giving its lay members a the-

ological outlook on life. We were giving a party a few months ago in the school. I happened to be about when the van bearing the meat pies drove in at the gate. The young man driving the van—an Afrikaner of, I suppose, twenty-five years of age—got out and asked me where he could deliver the meat pies. "What is this place?"

"An African secondary school, run by the Anglican mission."

"What do they learn here, these natives?"

"The same as European children: it was, in fact, the first African school in the Transvaal to reach Matric. standard."

"But what's the use? Isn't Dr. Verwoerd right in starting Bantu Education?"

I told the young man that as a result of "Bantu Education" St. Peter's school would soon be closing down. It was at that point that we began to talk theology. This young van driver was a devout member of his *kerk*. I can remember his exact words as he clinched his argument about *apartheid* and the necessity for segregation. "Our difference," he said, "is eschatalogical." I wondered how many Anglican van drivers, speaking incidentally in a foreign language, could have used that term so accurately. And he was right. Basically the Dutch Reformed Church cannot conceive of a relationship between black and white *in this world* which is in any sense real or tangible in terms of love. Perhaps at the end of time, in the last days (which is what eschatology means) it may be possible. "After this I beheld, and, lo, a great multitude which no man could number, of all nations, and kindreds, and peoples, and tongues, stood before the Throne, and before the Lamb. . . ." But there must not and cannot be any reflection of this vision in the congregations of God's children here on earth. "That they may be one, as Thou Father art in me and I in Thee, that the world may believe . . ." Our Lord's prayer for unity can have no reference to this world, even though the fulfilment of it would mean the world's believing. *Apartheid*—separation—here on earth: that is a precondition of eternal bliss hereafter. "The great gulf fixed" is an image of this world's heaven, not of the next world's hell.

It is essential to understand this fact about South African religion, even if it does not make it any easier to understand how such a religion squares with the Christian Gospel. It would, I think, be true to say that the Dutch Reformed Church has abandoned the attempt to find actual scriptural authority for the doctrine of *apartheid* other than the rather general argument about the Creation which I have tried to outline. But it is also true to say that the Dutch Reformed Church is the strongest exponent of "total *apartheid*" in this country. When at its Bloemfontein conference it expressed this view very clearly and went on to point out the logic of it—namely, that industry would have to do without black labour, that whites would have to do their own housework, that there would have to be a fresh approach to the land question— the government's reaction was immediate. Dr. Daniel Malan, Prime Minister and ex-predikant, dissociated himself entirely from this view of *apartheid* and affirmed with vigour that it was not the view of the Nationalist Party. In other words and in simple terms, the Dutch Reformed Church recognises that if there is to be a just *apartheid* (which indeed it fully believes in and hopes for), it must be total. In so far as the majority of leading Afrikaners are members of that church, they are bound to be greatly influenced by such a view. But for practical and political reasons the government cannot possibly act on such an

assumption. The Union is becoming increasingly industrialised and cannot find the labour, skilled or unskilled, to
meet its own development. The land set apart for purchase
to provide more Reserves, more purely "native areas," has
not yet been bought even to the limited extent planned.
It cannot be, because the European farmer is unwilling to
sell, and it is the European farmer's vote which counts for
most. So we have reached yet another paradox in this land
of paradox: those who desire *apartheid* from the best motives are opposed and thwarted in their plans for achieving
it by those who also desire it, but from the lowest and
least worthy. As always in a fallen world, it is the latter
group which is most numerous and most powerful.

If, then, the Dutch Reformed Church believes so
strongly in *apartheid,* why does it embark upon "missionary" work and what is the basis of such work? In the African Reserves as well as in the urban areas the Dutch
Reformed Church has for years both evangelised and provided schools and normal colleges. Many of these latter
are of as high a standard in building, equipment, and
staffing as any mission station in the country. And there
are white predikants working these missions. True, there
is never any intermingling of races either in worship or, so
far as that is possible, in work. True, the predikant on the
"mission ring" has a rather different status from his brother
who is engaged in white work. But, nevertheless, a great
deal of money is given by the European congregations to
the missions, a great deal of interest is taken in their work.
Why? To what end?

I had occasion recently to write to a Dutch Reformed
institution to ask them to receive and conduct a party of
American educationalists round their centre. In the letter
of reply the principal of the school wrote: "We shall be

66

very pleased to show these American tourists how much the whites are doing for the natives in South Africa."

I do not for one moment wish to impugn the sincerity or the devotion of the Dutch Reformed missionary. I have no doubt that his first purpose in undertaking the work or responding to the vocation which is his is to preach the Gospel, to teach his flock to know and love and serve Almighty God. But it is always with the conviction that somehow in the eternal purposes of Providence the white race is to *lead* the black: the black race is to depend upon, to look up to, to *need* the white. *Baasskap,* they call it. "Boss-ship"—"overlordship"—in spiritual as in material things, for ever and ever, amen. The only illogicality of it is that, with total *apartheid,* presumably the day must come and must be desired when black and white Christians have no earthly contact with each other at all. Then, one imagines, the African must still remember that there *are* white Christians, that their civilisation *is* superior to his, but that now it is out of his reach:

> *East is East, and West is West,*
> *And never the twain shall meet. . . .*

Perhaps even the bliss of heaven must depend upon some form of eternal *baasskap* shaded white. Everyone knows that the political influence of the Dutch Reformed Church (which incidentally is made up of three separate churches) is in South Africa very great indeed. By its insistence on the morality of segregation it makes a tremendously strong predisposing factor in the whole issue which confronts the country. It is not too much to say that it gives to *apartheid* exactly the religious sanction which the Christian Church everywhere else in the world gives to the idea that "all men are of equal value in the sight of

God." And so it was possible, at the World Council of Churches in 1954, for the South African representatives of the Dutch Reformed Church to withhold their assent from the declaration which affirmed any form of racial discrimination to be contrary to the will of God. They stood entirely alone in Christendom on this issue, separated even from their parent church in Holland.

The isolation of the church is echoed in the isolationism of South Africa herself. The bitter complaints that she is "misunderstood" at the U.N. and elsewhere are part of a whole attitude, an attitude very largely formed by the theological, or pseudo-theological, doctrines of a church entirely out of touch with the Christian world. It is this indeed which makes it so desperately difficult to find any common ground for the discussion of the racial "problem" in this country. For theological differences are notoriously the most difficult to resolve. When recently I was discussing the implications of the Bantu Education Act with one of the senior government officials in the department, I felt bound to say at the end of a long, friendly, but fruitless argument: "The truth is that we worship different Gods." I do not think I exaggerated.

But of course, though it is the largest single Christian body in *white* South Africa, the Dutch Reformed Church is not dominant in the country as a whole. The Methodist, the Anglican, the Roman Catholic, the Presbyterian—in fact, practically every Christian body in Christendom—is represented and, in the "mission field," very strongly represented. There should be no question of the power of their witness on the racial issues. Why, in fact, is it so ineffective? Why, in fact, does the European population of the Union, the English-speaking section especially, accept and live by the concept of *apartheid* if it is contrary to the teaching of the church or denomination to which it belongs? What is the matter with the witness of the Church here that it can influence policies so little?

I will not presume to criticise any Christian body other than the Anglican Church—the Church of the Province of South Africa, as it is officially called—to which I belong and of which I am a priest. This is not to suggest that the other Christian bodies are in no need of criticism, nor is it to suggest that the Anglican Church is especially blameworthy. I think it would be true to say that in outspokenness, in the utterances of her archbishops and bishops, in the published resolutions of her synods—the Church has been outstanding. But over the past twelve years, at any rate, this witness has been totally ineffective in its influence on the mass of white South Africa. I do not say that that is a reason for refraining from such utterance. "Whether they will hear, or whether they will forbear," the truth must be told, the voice must proclaim principles of justice and mercy and love. But I do say that it is not enough. And I do say also that within the Anglican Church as it exists in South Africa today there is enough colour prejudice, enough uncharitableness, and enough sheer blindness to lose it its influence over the African people in the next generation or less.

It is this sense of urgency which has led me to a position which I know to be in conflict with that of many leading Anglicans whose opinion I greatly respect and whose friendship I immensely value. It is difficult, looking back, to see exactly at what point one knows oneself to be making a new decision or taking a new road. All I can say is that over the years I took my share in framing and speaking to resolutions of Synod which condemned *apartheid* or which urged advance in opening up opportunity for

Africans or which called upon the government to redress obvious injustices. It was heartening to feel that those European lay folk, businessmen mostly, who attended Synod year by year could so readily be persuaded to vote the right way on racial issues. It was a comfort to imagine that they represented the ordinary South African "man in the street" and to believe that over the years their influence would prevail to break down these hideous barriers between man and man. It was only as the years slipped by that I began to wonder whether in fact it meant such things at all. Perhaps it was simply a matter of patience. That, anyhow, was what most bishops said, and clergy too. Perhaps it still is. But I do not believe it, and I cannot act or speak as if I did.

Strangely, it was an incident which in itself stood right outside the context of church affairs which I think forced me to a different view, shocked me into a new attitude, and brought me into some measure of conflict with ecclesiastical authority. The incident happened on a Sunday morning in Sophiatown two or three years ago.

Already the threat to remove the African people from that area had become a reality. A meeting of the residents was called, and I was asked to be one of the speakers. The Odin Cinema was chosen as the most suitable place for the purpose because it was in the very heart of Sophiatown and had seating for twelve hundred people. When after Mass I arrived in the vestibule, there was already a small group of Europeans, two or three men, arguing with some of the African and Indian delegates and claiming that as they were the C.I.D. they were entitled to come into the meeting. This I thought to be untrue, but to make quite sure I went into a neighbouring shop and rang up a lawyer friend of mine who confirmed my opinion. I then returned and asked the police to leave. They did so reluctantly; our meeting began, and the cinema auditorium was quite full.

Just after I had spoken there was a commotion at the door and a body of police strode in, marched quickly and with determination up the aisle and on to the stage, and arrested Yusuf Cachalia, a prominent Indian Congress leader. I would emphasise that the meeting itself was perfectly legal in every respect, and it was fully representative of the people of Sophiatown: those most deeply affected by the removal scheme. It was, in fact, one of the few opportunities available to them for expressing their views. Not unnaturally those views were strongly held and strongly expressed. To choose such a moment for the public arrest, in an atmosphere of tension, of Cachalia was, it seemed to me, quite criminal.

The people rose to their feet in the dark hall, twelve hundred of them, and made their anger known as the police hurried towards the exit. I was really frightened lest that anger should find expression in violence, and I followed the police and their prisoner. When we opened the door we were confronted with a policeman holding a tommy gun at the ready, several more police in the foyer with rifles, and, in the street immediately outside, a hundred or more African police armed. All this to arrest one man, who afterwards was released, as no charge could be laid against him. The people inside the cinema were in an angry mood and could very easily have rushed the doors—on to the tommy gun. It would have been a massacre. I protested to the officer in charge and was threatened with arrest myself. "If you will call off those police I will see that the meeting ends peacefully; otherwise I cannot be responsible for the consequences." Eventually the police drove away and we finished our meeting.

Again a simple enough incident and one which, I suppose, could be paralleled very easily in other countries. But I had seen and felt in those moments the terrifying spectre of the police state. It was all too much like Nazi Germany at its beginning. There was the fierce breath of totalitarianism and tyranny in every attitude, every movement of the police. . . .

I have attended many meetings since then at which the Special Branch of the C.I.D. has been present. But that Sunday morning at Sophiatown brought home to me as nothing else had done how very far along the road we had already travelled. Against this, Synod resolutions and episcopal utterances simply would not do. It seemed to me then, as it seems even more certain to me now, that the only way to meet this thing as a Christian was to try at least to arouse the Christian conscience throughout the world. For me, the arrest of Yusuf Cachalia, therefore, was significant far beyond itself. And from that day I have felt the need to use every means open to me of making known abroad, as well as within South Africa, the fearful lengths to which we have already gone in the suppression of personal liberties. It seemed to me then, as it seems to me at this moment, that the Church was largely unaware of all this or, if aware, was not prepared to take any strenuous action. But in appealing to the Christian conscience overseas, through the press, one immediately laid oneself open to attack as disloyal to South Africa. I cannot in fact accept that criticism, for I feel convinced that the Christian has a loyalty which stands above—far above—such considerations.

Apart from the need to arouse the Christian conscience in the world, there was in my heart, from that moment, in clear and unmistakable form, the desire to identify myself with the African people in their struggle for human rights and personal freedom. This I tried to express a little later at a meeting of the African National Congress in the city. But identification means more than words, more than speeches. For the Christian, so it seems to me, it is part of the life of faith itself. It is this mystery of identification which finds its very expression in the stable of Bethlehem: God, Almighty and Eternal, identifying Himself with man at his most helpless, with man in his utter littleness and poverty. Surely, if the Incarnation means anything at all, it must mean the breaking down of barriers not by words but by deed, by act, by *identification*. On Maundy Thursday, in the liturgy of the Catholic Church, when the Mass of the day is ended the priest takes a towel and girds himself with it; he takes a basin in his hands and, kneeling in front of those who have been chosen, he washes their feet and wipes them, kissing them also one by one. So he takes, momentarily, the place of his Master. The centuries are swept away, the Upper Room in the stillness of the night is around him: "If I, your Lord and Master, have washed your feet, ye also ought to wash one another's feet." I have knelt in the sanctuary of our lovely church at Rosettenville and washed the feet of African students, stooping to kiss them. In this also I have known the meaning of identification. The difficulty is to carry the truth out into Johannesburg, into South Africa, into the world.

The Episcopal Synod of the Church of the Province of South Africa meeting in 1954 put forward a statement in which the bishops said: "It has been stated that the fact that normally Europeans and Africans worship in different Church buildings is itself an acknowledgement of the principle of segregation. This is not so. Both linguistic and geographical reasons make it natural that normally Africans and Europeans should worship in different places. But an African member of the Church is at liberty to worship in any Church which he may desire and no one has any authority to exclude any Churchman of any race from any of our Churches, if he presents himself there for the purpose of worship." In other words, there is no colour bar in church.

Let us look at the facts. It is true, of course, that in any of the towns or cities the African people will live in locations apart from their European masters. And, obviously, if the Church is to do its job in caring for them, churches must be built in the locations and will therefore be "African" churches. But it is also true that in every large town there are thousands of African domestic servants who live where they work—in the back-yard rooms built on to every European house. These also are Christians. But it is rare indeed for them to attend church at the same time as their employers. Special services, at an early hour in the morning, are sometimes provided for them. They can meet together to worship the same God, to receive the same sacraments as the master and "missus," but not in the same service. And even this custom can sometimes cause difficulty, as it did when a young priest I know recently suggested to his Church Council that an "African" Mass might be allowed at 5:30 A.M. once a month or so in his church. Half the Council resigned in protest.

It would be true, I believe, to say that in the vast majority of Anglican parishes in European areas the presence in church of any number of Africans at any service would be greatly resented and would cause serious trouble. Only in the Cape, where there is a very large coloured population, are "mixed" congregations a regular feature of church life. It is true that on special occasions, such as an ordination or "Synod Sunday" in the cathedral, the pattern is different. Black and white are present and communicate together. It is true that in some parishes where the priest is courageous and alive to the situation some real progress is being made. But it is *not* true, and it is wrong to pretend that it is, that "geographical and linguistic" difficulties are the basic cause of these racial divisions within the Church. In the Church, as outside it, it is prejudice and fear and racialism itself which operate to confound the principles and ideals of episcopal pronouncements. Only if we face this fact and make no excuses can we hope to abolish the colour bar within the Church. But it is more than probable that in doing so we shall lose great numbers of our European Christians. It will be better so. For there is, in this matter especially, no time to lose. Already, in the African community, we are watching the emergence of a sectarian Christianity based partly on African nationalism, partly on a revolt against the disciples of organised Christianity, partly on the terrible example of disunity shown by white "churches" of many denominations. Moreover, in an increasingly secularised educational system, there is plenty of scope for that kind of pseudo-scientific attack on religion which is common to modern society everywhere. Young Africa is not immune. And when it is possible to point to a failure in Christian witness on the colour issue, as it most certainly is, then young Africa is alert to recognise such failure and by it to condemn the religion which allows it to happen.

It is, I think, significant that the Roman Catholic and Anglican missions in the urban areas of Johannesburg (and I presume in other cities also) have been alone in encouraging their European priests and religious to live within the area itself. Significant because in this way they have been able to share far more fully the problems and the pain of their people even if, by the accident of colour, they have not been able totally to identify themselves with them. It is significant, too, because there has been far less breaking away, far less schismatic division in these two bodies than in the Protestant denominations, which generally rely on African ministers, supervised from outside by European superintendents.

The point I am trying to make is a very simple one, yet I think it needs making in every possible way. *It is that the Church is facing a challenge which it must meet now and which it cannot meet effectively with official pronouncements alone.* Only the white Christians of South Africa can truly meet that challenge; not the bishops, not the clergy, but the ordinary lay folk who *are* the Church. And I do not believe that they are meeting it; I do not believe that they really know a challenge exists. In fact, the most disheartening thing about the Christian situation in this country is the absence of any deep sense of urgency. It is not that white Christians are bad, very far from it. It is simply that they fail to see the relevance of their faith to social problems. Just as in the England of Wilberforce there were those who defended slavery from the highest motives; just as there were, in the time of the Industrial Revolution, Christian leaders who acquiesced in child labour in the cotton mills and all the other horrifying evils which Charles Dickens exposed—so in South Africa there is an apathy and a patience within the Church towards the evil of racialism which is harder to bear and far more difficult to break through than deliberate malice and wickedness.

It is not easy to condemn *apartheid* and the doctrine of white supremacy in the state if it exists and is suffered to exist within the Church. The answer to the question: Will the African remain Christian in the years to come? depends more than anything else on the answer made to the vital question of colour within the Church *now*. So I return to that incident in the long history of the Church, a moment when the wrong answer would have in fact destroyed it as the instrument of God's love to all men. St. Paul withstood St. Peter "to the face" over the issue of the admission of the Gentiles. He won his point. Had he not done so, the Christian Church would have remained a Jewish sect and presumably would have died, as other sects have died, many centuries ago in the hinterland of Antioch or Rome. It is this sense of urgency which has led me to believe that the only effective weapon to use is the conscience of Christendom itself; that it is not wrong, therefore, to appeal to Christians the world over to condemn racial discrimination wherever it exists. When in the early thirties the Nazis began to persecute the Jews, the official voice of the Church was silent. The Niemollers and the Faulhabers called too late upon the Christian world. After all, a modern state has every propaganda instrument at its command; the Church has the voice and the pen of its leaders alone.

I have become convinced that *within* South Africa, it is now impossible to mobilise a sufficiently powerful offensive to counteract the forces which operate so strongly, so subtly, and so irrationally against us. Indeed, sometimes it is desperately hard not to be caught up oneself in the toils of the situation, not to wonder whether one is oneself utterly mistaken in trying to swim against the tide. Perhaps this book of mine may bring some answer and some comfort, or at least the reassurance which one longs for in loneliness. But whether it does or not, I must clear my own conscience. This does not mean the condemnation of others who think and act and speak differently. I do not for one moment question the integrity of their faith. But for me there is only one really vital issue confronting the Church in South Africa, and I do not think the Church is facing it as boldly as it should, as it *must*, if it is to be true to its Master and to itself. Idealism, like patriotism, is not enough.

V. The *Tsotsi*

Others may sing of the wine and the wealth and
the mirth,
The portly presence of potentates goodly in girth;—
Mine be the dirt and the dross, the dust and scum
of the earth!

JOHN MASEFIELD, *"A Consecration"*

"HEY THERE, *tsotsi*, show me your pass. . . ."

The boy stopped. He had a parcel in one hand and it
wasn't easy to get the book quickly enough—luckily he had
it on him. The policeman did not even look inside it. But
when Joel came to see me it was the abusive term, the contemptuous title, *tsotsi*, that had made its mark—more
surely, too, than a cuff on the ear or a twist of the arm. For
as it happened, Joel was already near the top of Form
Three, and the European constable who had stopped him
had probably left school after the primary standard six.
At least that is all that is required of police constables in
South Africa. That is why so often their venom is directed
at the "educated kaffir," the "cheeky nigger," the "smart
skellum." And it is not only the police who think that way,
of course. There was an instance not so long ago when an
African, standing at a bus stop (second class) dared to put
on a pair of white gloves. This was so offensive to a group
of European lads waiting for their bus (first class) nearby

79

that they set on him, had him down in the gutter, and kicked him so that he died.

"*Tsotsi*"—what does it mean? It is a familiar enough name in every urban African township, familiar enough to have become a term of abuse when applied by a European to an educated African, a term of contempt tinged with fear when used by one African boy of another. Yet it means something of quite tremendous importance to all those whose job is to care for the young of Christ's flock. Every country in its large cities has its "cosh-boys," its "wide-guys," its "gangsters," its "Teddys." And the *tsotsi*, the real genuine *tsotsi*, is all of these, though first and foremost he is just a boy. The origin of the name is interesting, for it is a corruption of "zoot suit," and the *tsotsi*, like the Teddy-boy, is supposedly characterised by the cut of his clothes. In this case, because not many African youngsters can claim to have clothes which are "cut," the tight-fitting drainpipe trousers are the distinctive mark. But today in Alexandra and Sophiatown and Pimville and Moroka it is not the clothes, it is the number, the gang, the weapons which are so terrifyingly evident. The *tsotsi* is youth rotting away and rotting with fear the society around him. He is problem number one in urban Africa.

One Saturday evening in Sophiatown I was on the *stoep* of the mission house after Evensong and Rosary. A boy came running across the school playground, one of the servers. "It's the principal, Father, come please quickly, he's been stabbed. . . ." I got someone to help me with the stretcher (we always kept it handy and often had to use it) and went as quickly as I could, the boy directing me, to a house hard by the school. Elias Mokoetsi lay on the *stoep*, unconscious and with blood staining his open shirt. There was little excitement. We got him on to the stretcher and down to the clinic. The doctor gave him an injection. There was one tiny wound in the breast, no more than a quarter of an inch long. But it was enough, for it was just over his heart. He died within ten minutes. On Sunday after High Mass a woman asked to see me; with her was a young lad of nineteen, who said, "I've come to give myself up to you, Father. I stabbed the principal. I didn't mean to kill him, Father. He hit me and I got mad. I had a knife. . . ."

One evening I was driving back from preaching to a European congregation on the other side of the town. It was a winter evening also, and at ten o'clock at night there were not many people about. I was tired, thankful to be getting back to the mission and to bed, not thinking about much else, I expect. But as I drove along the main road which makes the boundary of Sophiatown and Martindale, I saw under a lamppost a man lying in the dust. He was close to the tram lines. There was no one near him. Almost I drove on. Drunks on Sunday night were not uncommon in that part of the world, and I was tired. But something, perhaps Someone, made me stop and get out of the car and go to him to try to help him. He was dead. This time it was a bicycle spoke with one end sharpened which had pierced his heart.

Alfred Vukela was one of those lads whom one could only possibly describe as "vital." He had been a server for many years, ever since he was a child. But he was not at all the copybook type of altar boy. Indeed, I have never known an African who was. Amongst other things, he belonged to a concert party which specialised in hot jazz and jiving, in tap dancing and all the rest. In this way he added a little to his earnings. He was in a good job, and his boss was really fond of him. He had just married, and his wife had had her first baby. He was walking home one night with a friend when he suddenly heard someone behind him. Before he could even turn round he felt a blow between the shoulder blades and a sharp pain. When he came to, he found he was flat on the ground; he could not get up, he could not move his legs. He had been stabbed in the back, and a motor nerve had been cut. Today, three years later, he still sits in a room somewhere in the back of Sophiatown. He will not jive again.

I have given these three illustrations because they are the ones that come most readily to mind; not, alas, because they are the only incidents I can remember of the terrible and terrifying destructiveness of the *tsotsi*.

Woven into the whole pattern of fear, which is the pattern of so much of South Africa's life, is this fear which is ever present in the locations and townships of the Reef. And it is a by-product of a whole attitude of mind, of something which could undoubtedly be cured if it were not for the irrational and morbid obsession over colour which so entirely petrifies constructive work in the social field. For the *tsotsi* is symbolic of something other than a simple social evil, common to all countries. He is, I believe, more than a juvenile delinquent, more than a "case" for an approved school. Like them, he is aggressively anti-social; but, unlike them, he has a profound reason, as a rule, for being so. He is the symbol of a society which does not care. He is in revolt against the frustration which apparently cannot be cured, cannot be relieved. He turns upon his own people and uses his knife against them because he is caught in that trap from which there is no escape—the trap which Nature seems to have set for him by giving him a black skin. Alan Paton, in his picture of Absalom, has given one story of the typical *tsotsi* boy. But it is not the only one; it is not the most common. Absalom comes up from the country to find his sister and is caught in the life of the city, bewildered by it, his standards destroyed by it, and he himself eventually becomes the criminal and the victim of it. No doubt there are many such. But the *tsotsi* I know best has never set foot in the country. He is a "cockney" by birth, and so, possibly, are his parents before him. The only life he knows is the life of the town. The only standards he recognises are those provided by an urban, industrialised society. He would be as much a stranger in the *kraals* of Zululand as I would be in Tibet. What is it, then, which makes him what he is? How can it be that that lovely little boy of six, with the sparkling eyes and the friendly smile, has become a killer at sixteen? And how is it that there are so many like him? So many that, in the most modern location in South Africa, people are scared to go out of their homes at night except in groups.

In the first place, it must be recognised that social welfare work in South Africa amongst Africans is hamstrung from the first not so much by lack of money as by the attitude of mind which racialism inevitably produces. The most common phrase, I suppose, in use in this country is "the native problem." By this phrase everything is summed up. It is an abstraction—and so, to the average white man, is the African. It is a "problem"—never an opportunity. In some strange way one has to avoid thinking of black men as if they were persons at all. And so the *tsotsi* is just part of this great abstraction too. He is not a boy who has gone wrong; he is a native "skellum." He doesn't belong to a family with a father and mother and brothers and sisters— he is a "problem." White society has to solve the "problem" if it can, because crime is an expensive and unedifying commodity. But white society should not be asked to take a personal interest in it, still less provide money for its solution—for it lies altogether outside the sphere of human relations. It belongs to that other world, which it is easiest to forget. This was brought home to me very forcibly by the murder of Elias Mokoetsi and by another incident which I shall try to describe.

When it became known that Elias had been stabbed to death for no reason, the people of Sophiatown were fiercely angry. He had been one of the most respected men in the township: he had taught their children for many years; he was a gentleman. When his funeral took place some six thousand people turned out to show how they honoured him. As on so many occasions in my life in Sophiatown, I felt a great sense of pride that in all that crowd I, a white man, was allowed to perform the last rites. My priesthood was so much more important than my colour. After it was all over a deputation came to the mission and asked me to arrange a meeting with the police. The people, they said, were determined to protect themselves if the police could not or would not protect them. During the war, when European policemen had joined the forces and were in short supply, there had been an African Civic Guard. It was this which they wished to revive. We had the meeting a few days later, and Colonel X., commandant of the district, arrived with some subordinates to hear what the deputation wanted.

An old Zulu who had lived in the area for many years stood up and put the case strongly yet with courtesy. "Our people know the criminals better than the police can do. When the police come the people are fearful; they even hide the *tsotsis*. They fear the police more than they fear the *tsotsis*. But we know where they stay. We are not satisfied that the police protect us. . . ."

Colonel X. called for his record books. "Now look, man," he said, "let us take the year 1942. In that year there was a Civic Guard in Sophiatown. In the month of March there were only . . . there were only . . ." He paused and prepared himself to make a startling pronouncement. "Only *twelve* arrests." He turned to the old Zulu. "What is the use of a Civic Guard if it can only arrest twelve people in a month?"

"I think," said the Zulu, "that it shows that the Civic Guard was doing its job."

To Colonel X., however, the only criterion of police efficiency was in the number of arrests made. It did not matter that 70 per cent would be for pass offences, not for crime at all. So we did not get our Civic Guard then or ever, and the *tsotsis* continued to flourish in the dark streets and in the back yards which the police dared not try to reach. Incidentally, when Elias Mokoetsi's murderer was tried it was discovered that he had six previous convictions, several of them of a serious nature, although he was only nineteen. The charge was reduced to culpable homicide. He was sentenced to one year in jail. So far as I know, he is still walking the streets of Sophiatown. After all, it was only another stabbing in a native area, part of the "problem." Why worry too much? Neither the boy who murdered nor the man who was murdered had real value as a person. Both were natives: a different category, another species living in a world apart.

The second incident was this. I remember sitting in my office one Saturday morning when I heard a noise of running and a hoarse voice shouting in Afrikaans words which I could not distinguish but which were words of anger. In the garden outside the front door some six or seven boys were standing together, and a young European constable, his hand on his revolver, was bawling at them and was obviously in a furious rage. "What it's all about?" I asked.

"These boys—where are their passes?"

I told him that they were schoolboys, home for the holidays, all known to me, and I asked him to get out of the mission. With the help of one of my colleagues I took his number and went, not very hopefully, to report the incident to the senior officer at the station. Not long afterwards, the answer to the inquiry that I had asked for was brought to me at the mission by Captain E., an English-speaking police officer whom I had met before. It was his day off, and he was not very pleased at having to spend part of it on the job. The reason for the incident, he explained, was that the constable had been chasing a suspect and thought he might have taken refuge in the mission. "But anyway, Father, you know yourself that 70 per cent of the people in this place are criminals." I suggested that if that was the official attitude of the police they were not very likely to win the trust and confidence of Sophiatown.

It was, to me at least, an interesting comment on the whole sad situation. Just one more indication of the same basic mental attitude. The native is a problem; he is never a person. He is, more often than not, a criminal who cannot be trusted even if he is apparently only a schoolboy. You must bawl at him, threaten him, handcuff him—that is the treatment he really understands. And if it is not enough, there is always the sjambok. It will be said that this is an exaggeration. I only wish it were. I have told it as accurately as I can remember it, not because as was once said to me, "You hate the uniform of the South African police," but because I know that this attitude is in itself a reason for the *tsotsi*. It is not the only reason, but it is a very fundamental one; and it is expressive, I think, of that whole mental attitude which belongs to white South Africa.

In a recent comprehensive survey of one of the African townships it was discovered (though those of us who lived there knew it from firsthand experience) that the average family had to face a gap between income and expenditure of over two pounds ten shillings per month. How is this gap to be closed? In the answer to that question there lies another answer to the reason for the *tsotsi*. It is poverty. In Johannesburg more than half the total population of the city is non-European. Apart from those thousands of migrant labourers employed by the mines and living in compounds, quite separate from the locations of the city, there are at least 350,000 Africans who belong to Johannesburg and upon whose labour Johannesburg depends. Taking the survey I have referred to as an accurate index (and I have every reason to believe that it is), it would not be an exaggeration to say that at least half the African families in the city must live below the bread line—UNLESS THEY CAN CLOSE THAT GAP.

African families—thank God—are large as a rule. The average number of children in a family is anything between four and seven. Quite often it is more. So, clearly, if they are to be fed and clothed, it is necessary for both parents to go out to work. With their strong sense of "family," this is an unnatural and most undesirable thing for the African people. But it is nowadays an accepted thing also. And it might be all right if there were compulsory education, if the parents could be sure that their children were in school whilst they were out at work. That is the one thing they cannot be sure of. In the urban areas about one child in three can find a place in school. The remaining two thirds of the child population has only the street or the empty room for its long day. And in places like Sophiatown or Alexandra Township that is not so good.

"Father, I've come to give you my child, you must take care of him. Father—he is naughty, very, very naughty. I can do nothing with him. He dodges school. He is a 'loafer.' He stays out at night. . . ." How often I have heard these words? And they are spoken over the head of a child of eight or ten. He is "out of control." And he really *is* out of control. I know that the chances are that he is already with a gang. Probably he has taken part in quite a few minor burglaries—fruit or sweets or cigarettes from the "China" shops. When I look down at him I can see a hardness already forming round his mouth, in his eyes. And there is so little I can hope to do. "Father must get him to school." But all the schools are full and overfull. "Father must send him away from Johannesburg to a boarding school." But there are no boarding schools for boys of his age and of his standard in education. "Father must take him to Diepkloof" (the reformatory which Alan Paton once supervised and from which he learnt about Absalom and old Kumalo)—but Diepkloof already has seven hundred boys and in any case cannot take any boy unless he is committed by a magistrate.

There is too much competition; there are too few probation officers. Above all, there are too few people who even begin to care. Sometimes in Johannesburg at night when the cinema crowds are flooding out on to the pavements I have watched African children—some of them certainly not more than eight years old—hanging about the lighted entrances, darting through the legs of the emerging throng, watching the Greek shops with their brilliant windows. They are filthy dirty. They are hungry. They hold out their hands—"Penny, *baas*, penny, *baas*"—and sometimes they get what they ask and run off in search of more. But nobody cares what happens to them or from where they come. Nobody cares that these children, who belong to someone, somewhere, will soon be in those same Johannesburg streets with knives or with stolen revolvers; will be, in fact, the *tsotsis* of tomorrow. White South Africa lives in fear, but it does surprisingly little to remove the causes. It prefers burglarproofing, private watchmen, the revolver by the bedside to any kind of constructive approach to the problem of the *tsotsi*. And if half the money which is spent on keeping pass offenders in prison were spent instead on building schools or equipping boys' clubs, the crime wave would soon become less menacing.

There is, however, another cause of "*tsotsi*-ism." It is illegitimacy. And this is also something which white South Africa views with a sickening complacency and with a pharisaical shrug of the shoulders. "These kaffirs. Breed like rabbits." Or, "My 'girl' has a lot of boy friends, of course. But what can you do? It's their nature." Or, "She's pregnant again. She'll have to go. I can't have an infant in the house. What a nuisance these girls are. I'd almost sooner do the work myself." Or, more rarely on the telephone, "Father, I don't know you and you don't know me. I've got a girl here, and we've had her working for us for a long time. Now she's got two children and they're growing up. I can't keep them in the servant's room. Is there a school or an institution? . . . Nothing? . . . Oh, but surely there's *some* place. . . . I thought you'd be sure to know of somewhere. . . . Can't you help at all?" No, I cannot. I cannot because the thing is far too big, and its roots go far too deep in the rottenness of a social order which white South Africa tolerates and, more than tolerates, desires. I cannot, because in the whole Union there is only one institution that will take pregnant African girls and their babies, and that is always overfull. I am its chairman, and I know. I cannot, because you, the "missus," accept your servant for the work she will do; you do not give a thought to where she comes from, how she lives, or what she needs in the way of protection. You say (how many hundred times have I heard you?) that you do everything for her and she is ungrateful. What you mean is that you pay her her wages, give her enough to eat, sometimes give her clothing which you can no longer wear yourself. But what of her life in that back room at the bottom of your yard, completely separate (by law) from the house? That is, for the time being, her home. The door does not lock properly and the windows are not barred. There is no security.

In the white suburbs of Johannesburg there are thousands of African servants of both sexes. They must live sufficiently close to their work to be on call six days out of seven and seven nights out of seven. But they must live in *kayas*—single rooms of varying quality built away from the house. There are no recreation centres of any kind in any of the European suburbs for African servants. From time to time attempts have been made by small groups of liberal-minded people to do something about this. On every occasion the attempt has been defeated. "It will bring down the value of our property. It will bring in all the natives from the next suburb. It will encourage crime."

Not so long ago we had seven acres of land next door to our priory in Rosettenville, today a European suburb, though when we chose it for our mission it was in open country, miles from the centre of the city. We could not use this land as a football field for our schoolboys, though we should have liked to do so. It was coveted by our European neighbours for the valuable site that it could be.

We offered it to the City Council of Johannesburg to be used as a recreation centre for the African domestic servants in the neighbourhood, sixteen thousand of them. The offer was made public. Immediately a Vigilance Committee was formed. Meetings were held throughout the suburb. A petition with two thousand signatories was organised. We were told that all our windows would be broken and our priory attacked if we proceeded with the plan to sell. I was present at the meeting in the City Hall when the Vigilance Committee made its formal protest to the City Council. "Three hundred natives are imported every day by bus into the priory. It is a hide-out for criminals." It was only an official visit by the city councillors concerned which prevented the matter going any further— that and our decision, in the interest of our own continued existence as a mission, not to press the issue.

Indeed nothing can so swiftly arouse the wrath of white suburbia as a plan for providing African servants with recreational facilities. Protest meetings are planned with great swiftness and are attended in force. The English immigrant who has, for the first time in his life, a servant and a car is perhaps more ready to support such a protest than his Afrikaner neighbour. But both are united in a fierce determination to prevent their suburb becoming attractive to the native servant they employ. So, in fact, the "girl" or the "garden-boy" live in their separate rooms. But they do not always, in the hours when their work is done, stay by themselves or sleep alone. And their employers do not care what goes on, provided that it does not involve a police raid, provided that the morning tea is brought in on time, provided there is no "cheekiness."

What it really means is easy to understand. It means that Eva, who has a home in Sophiatown, or Grace, who lives in Orlando, soon has a babe in her womb, loses her job, returns disgraced to her family—and there is another child whose father is unknown, another child who, in all probability, Granny will have to look after, another child who, in the coming years, may be "nobody's business." These are the children who run the streets when they ought to be in school—if they could get into school. These are the *tsotsis* of tomorrow. And white South Africa shrugs its shoulders and complains that servants are not what they used to be. Nobody cares. Except, of course, the municipal authorities and the government. But they care in a strange and cynical way. They are determined, for instance, that the life of domestic servants shall be regulated and controlled. There must be an absolute enforcement of the law of registration. The moral law is another matter altogether. So we have reached the stage, in white Johannesburg, where a man and his wife, married by Christian rites, may not live together as man and wife unless they work for the same employer. "Whom God hath joined together, let no man put asunder . . ." but don't dare to go and visit each other; don't be discovered together in the same room or you are liable to arrest for trespass.

Is it so very surprising if a child, conceived and born in illegality, technically nonexistent, according to the law of the land a trespasser from birth, becomes in later life a rebel against society, black and white? I do not claim that every lad who becomes a *tsotsi* begins his life in this fashion; nor do I believe that it is environment alone which makes the criminal. There is such a thing as evil; there is sin in a fallen world. But I do not exaggerate when I say that the *tsotsi* is a symbol of society which does not care. And against that dead, oppressive weight of apathy it is so hard to make progress. It would be enough to make any priest despair unless he really believed that in the one or two who by the grace of God he has rescued there is his reward. And even then it is hard to be patient and to persevere.

It is often said, and with some truth, that the African in the towns has lost all the old tribal sanctions and nothing has been put in their place. It is also true, however, that some of the old customs, transplanted from country to town, have an equally disastrous effect. So it is with *lobola* —the dowry custom. The young man, before he can marry the girl of his choice, must in the country produce a certain number of cattle and hand them over (or see that his parents do so) to the parents of the bride. In this way her "value" and her security against ill treatment are safeguarded. There is an obvious and real point in this, and it is akin to many similar customs in other parts of the world. But in the towns the cattle becomes money. The parents of the girl demand thirty, sixty, or one hundred pounds. The boy has to earn or borrow this money. The marriage is often delayed unreasonably by the exorbitant demands made by the parents, with the result that the boy and girl anticipate their marriage, and one more illegitimate child is born.

It is a subject which is often under debate in missionary conferences and the like. On the whole, the conservative view prevails, the view of ancient custom. But the younger generation of African town dwellers is getting impatient and resentful, and probably a change will come. Nevertheless, in looking at the *tsotsi* problem as dispassionately as one can, the boy-girl question looms very large. It is precisely what one would expect, but no less difficult to deal with for all that. And some of the most vicious and mean of *tsotsi* crimes, assault on young girls, rape, and stabbing, are the result of this unresolved conflict produced by a society in transition between the old and the new. Yet, in seeing the *tsotsi* simply as a menace, we are not going to do very much to solve the problem of his existence. Behind the menace there is the frustration, the sense of impotence, the misdirected energy. And often enough there is a real initiative which can and should be used for good.

Together with the lack of schools, there is in the urban areas of our cities a fearful lack of recreational facilities. Every European suburb has its playground, its football fields, its tennis courts, its golf course, its swimming bath. For the African, the most he can expect is a football field or two, generally without any proper provision for spectators. Beyond that he has the street or the open, barren veldt, and he must use it as he can.

I remember in Sophiatown one of our young altar boys named Tom. Every afternoon when school was over he disappeared. On Saturday he was away all day—and sometimes on Sunday too. After a while I discovered that he had somehow got himself a golf club and a few balls. By caddying at the weekends he not only earned a little money and bought his equipment, but he also watched the players and learnt golf from them. He and the other lads would mark out a "course" on the stretch of rough, tussocky grass which lies between Sophiatown and the European suburb of Westdene. There they would play every afternoon. They still do. But there is no provision anywhere, so far as I know, for African golfers, except on the links of their own making. There are twelve public swimming baths and three thousand private pools in Johannesburg for the white population. For the Africans there are three, and only one of those (whose origin I shall describe in another chapter) is really a public bath.

I suppose that no single sporting event so strengthened white South Africa's respect for the African athlete as Jake Tuli's boxing triumph when he became flyweight champion of the Empire. Jake is an Orlando boy. He had to learn his boxing where all Orlando boys learn it, in one of the many clubs which flourish there and which flourish in every location and township in South Africa. But gymnasium space is generally an old, disused garage, or a corrugated-iron shed, or just the open space behind someone's house. There are, I know, many potential boxing champions, but they are not allowed to box against white opponents. It was bad enough when on one occasion a European boxer of world class was knocked out in a sparring bout, and it was revealed two days later that his partner was an African.

My point is this, and it is so obvious as hardly to be worth making: the *tsotsi* is very largely the product of frustration. And much of that frustration is physical: the absence of any decent, healthy outlet for his energies in recognised sport. It is something of a paradox that South Africa, which has such a reputation as a sporting country, should so limit its own possibilities by refusing to encourage the African in a field where he, too, can excel. It is tragic that by its needlessness and lack of imagination it is in fact adding just one more cause for fear to the many that exist already.

But in the final analysis none of the things I have tried to express is the cause of the *tsotsi*. The *tsotsi* is, first and foremost, a person, a boy who began life on the same terms and with the same background as the majority of African boys. Sometimes his home was bad: he was neglected or treated cruelly; sometimes his home was good: he was spoilt, left to go his own way, went "into a far country, and wasted his substance," like the Prodigal in the parable.

95

But, if that were all, he would be no more of a problem than the juvenile delinquent in every city in every country in the world.

In South Africa, in the urban area, in location and township, at the corners of every street and lurking in every dark alley, he *is* the youth of that place. Or, if that is an exaggeration, he is far too noticeable a feature of African urban life. He is not the exception but the rule. And the only remedy the government can think of is to pick him up, charge him under one or another section of the Native Urban Areas Act, and deport him to work as a farm labourer. Labour is cheap that way. It is popular, too, with the electorate. Work colonies are also being started for the same purpose. The assumption is that the *tsotsi* is a "won't-work," a loafer, who has no place in the cities. It is a convenient assumption, but is it true? I have said that I regard the *tsotsi* as a symbol—as the symbol of a rotten social order, corrupted through and through by the false ideology of racialism, of *apartheid*, of white supremacy. It is because for the African boy there is no future, no fulfilment beyond that of unskilled labour, or the "tea-boy" job in an office, or in the endless subservience of the shop or the factory; it is because of this that the African boy becomes a *tsotsi*.

David, aged twenty-three, had been a qualified teacher until the passing of the Bantu Education Act, when he felt in conscience that he must leave the profession. I managed to get him a job in the packing department of a great store. After about three weeks I called him to see me and asked how he was getting on. He did not find it easy to talk. He felt, no doubt, that as I had got him the job he would be a disappointment to me if he confessed to hating it. But in the end he said, quite simply and without any bitterness,

"It's all right, Father, except for that European lady. Sometimes, when I have to shift boxes or bales and put them on the counter, I have to move an account sheet or a weigh-bill from one place to another. Then she shouts at me, 'Don't touch that paper! Paper work is white work, it's not for natives.'"

"There is no place," says Dr. Verwoerd, "for the native in European society above the level of certain forms of labour." We need him for our industry. We need him for our national economy. We need him for our very existence as a country. But we do not need him for himself. We do not need him as a person who has life in front of him—life stretching down the years and needing colour and warmth and light, the colour and warmth and light of fulfilment and purpose. Sooner than grant him this we are prepared to watch him rot away morally, spiritually, physically even, in our rich and splendid cities. The *tsotsi* is the supreme symbol of a society which does not care. His knife and his revolver are significant not only for today but for tomorrow. But to me he is also a boy; he is David and John and Israel and Jonas and Peter. And for him and the use that he makes of life I shall one day have to answer before the judgment seat of God. I cannot cease to care.

VI. Shanty Town

Yet nightly pitch my moving tent
A day's march nearer home.
JAMES MONTGOMERY

NEWCLARE IS a straggling suburb separated from Sophiatown by the main road which runs through the city to the
Western Areas and beyond them to the Reef towns of
Roodepoort and Krugersdorp. And, although it is so much
a part of Sophiatown, it has a character of its own; a different atmosphere hangs like the smoke from its thousand
braziers over the squalid houses and over the "smart"
homes which stand side by side in its unplanned and un-
charted streets.

You can go down any street in Newclare and suddenly,
without warning and without reason, find that it has pe-
tered out into a field, grimy and grey, but still—a field. Or
you can walk down a narrow alley between houses and discover an open yard with a row of rooms facing it, doors
open or half shuttered with old packing cases to keep the
children in, a single latrine, a single tap, and twenty families making their own community in that restricted and
narrow plot. Moreover, they will be laughing as they hang
out the washing. The sickly sweet smell of "kaffir beer"
will certainly pervade the yard, and in a corner of it the
brown, dry "sawdust" which is the aftermath of brewing.

Or you will find in Newclare a gleaming shop front with chromium window bars and fluorescent lighting, with bales of silk and satin shining on the shelves and the Indian owner behind the counter expressive of the very essence of salesmanship.

We wanted a site for our little Church of St. Francis some years ago, and the only plot we could get was at the end of a long causeway on a rubbish dump. The church had to be built on concrete "stilts," and in consequence its floor seems to swing and sway as the congregation moves during Mass. On one corner of the township stands the great block of Coronation Hospital, a massive brick building which dominates the scene. Below it is the main railway line, running through a cutting and making a barrier between Newclare North and Newclare South. The way from one part to the other lies over a single bridge.

There is another characteristic of the place that you cannot miss if you are at all familiar with South Africa. It is that a great number of the inhabitants, both male and female, wear, over their ordinary clothes, gay blankets. They stand in the doorways, the red or green or blue blankets thrown loosely over the shoulder and pinned on one side. They are Basotho. In the country from which they come every store stocks this special and peculiar dress; every person, man, woman, and child, wears it. It is striking when you see it for the first time, and there is a gaiety about the colours and the patterns which could never have been thought of when the first skins of animals were replaced by the products of Witney and elsewhere. Newclare has a large Basotho colony, and much of it has been urbanised over the years and is a permanent part of the total population. The blankets even seem a little more sombre, a little more utilitarian than the gaudy things you see against the mountains of Basutoland itself.

In February 1950, Newclare was troubled. There was an uneasy and indefinable tension in the place; something was stirring beneath that strange surface of slum and open space, in those crowded back yards. It broke one weekend in riots. Indian shops were set on fire and looted. There were fierce clashes with the police who had been sent in to deal with the situation. Men were killed, some by bullets, some by stones. The House of Assembly began to take notice. The Minister of Justice ordered strong police action. There were ugly rumours that an attempt, deliberately planned by a small section of Europeans, had been made to stir up racial strife between Indian and African, to repeat the horrors of the Durban riots, to make it obvious that Newclare and the Western Areas in general were a threat to the peace of the city. After a month or two of such open violence, things calmed down again. Police patrols were much more evident, and Sten guns had become a familiar sight at the bridge between North and South.

Then suddenly again in March 1952 the whole area flared up. There was a pitched battle one evening that month; the combatants were all Africans; eleven were killed and ninety-five injured. It was hard to see what was happening or why anything was happening at all. Gradually the true picture emerged and was clarified. A Basotho gang, calling themselves the "Russians" (but having nothing whatever to do with the Communist party anywhere), had entrenched itself in Newclare South, across the railway line. It operated in strength every weekend, and its menacing existence made life impossible as soon as darkness fell. Its purpose was simple and its methods effective.

It offered its "protection" to the people of Newclare below the bridge—for a fee. If you refused to be "protected" you were threatened; if you refused to yield to threats you were attacked: attacked coming home in the twilight from work, crossing an open space or even, sometimes, when you went into your own yard. And somehow or other the police were never there when the "Russians" were active, or they came when the immediate trouble was over.

Newclare South seemed defenceless against this frightening and fantastic blanketed army of thugs. Authority ignored every plea from the people, threatened and fearful in their homes. Their only hope was self-protection. A Civil Guard was formed in Newclare North. Men, armed with heavy sticks and moving only in groups of a dozen or so, patrolled the streets after sundown. During the week at least a measure of security was achieved. But at the weekend it was much more difficult. Then the "Russians" were out in force, made deliberate raids wherever they could, and seemed to be able to get away without trouble. The Civil Guard redoubled its efforts. People in Sophiatown and its neighbouring townships were thankful to find that at night they, too, could move about the streets more freely. Once again an appeal was made to the authorities to allow recognition of the Guard. It was in fact essential, if the Guard was to continue, that it should have some official status such as it had enjoyed in the war years. There were already signs that it might otherwise be used itself as a cover for criminal activity.

In the meanwhile the weekend clashes in Newclare continued and became more bloody. Domestic servants did not turn up for work in the European suburbs, because they refused to risk the danger of attack by the gangsters. Their employers became interested in the whole situation for the first time. The municipality made special regulations for its white social workers. But still, for some strange reason which has remained unexplained to this day, the police did not disarm the "Russians." Sisters and nurses at the Coronation Hospital could watch the fighting from their windows, which looked across towards the bridge. They reported that when the clashes occurred and the police intervened it was not the gangsters who were disarmed but their opponents. How true that was I would not know. What I do know is that in March the Civil Guard was declared illegal and wound up.

Two months after that, conditions in South Newclare had become so impossible that people began to move out of their homes and to erect shacks and shelters in the open, over the bridge where at least they were among friends. They chose a vacant plot on a corner named Plot 99 or "Reno Square," opposite one of the few African cinemas. It was a plot which for some purpose or other, long since forgotten, had been meant for shops and houses but had remained empty whilst the crowded streets surrounding it had filled up through the years. It was the size of a football field. Within a week two hundred families—about fifteen hundred people—were living there and overflowing on to another piece of land, known as the Charles Phillips Square. This was a far larger open space, as near as anything in an African area could be to a playground for the children—only it had no swings or seesaws, just a public lavatory in one corner and an iron fence all round it.

On July 2 the City Council and the police conferred and decided that they must forcibly evict the squatters. I had already spoken to the mayor on the telephone, and as a result of this I was asked to see what I could do to persuade the squatters to go back to their homes and face the

"Russians." The alternative to this was that they should be deported to a place called Hammanskraal, fifty miles away beyond Pretoria and in open country. I went as swiftly as I could to the camp, taking with me W. B. Ngakane, the field officer for the South African Institute of Race Relations. It was a very tough proposition: to persuade people who had been terrorised out of their homes that they must either walk back into the terror or be exiled.

As we drove out to Newclare, Ngakane was almost in tears. "It is impossible, Father, impossible! What have these poor people done? It isn't their fault. It's these 'Russians.' We know that the Basutoland Government has files full of evidence against their leaders. They are criminals, gangsters . . . they should be deported."

I decided that instead of going to Newclare I would go to Pretoria, interview the protectorates' authorities, and see what they knew. It seemed simply hopeless to try to do anything else. I was confident that the squatters would not move, even under threat of eviction and deportation, even though it was the beginning of a high-veldt winter and their only protection was a hessian sack stretched across two sticks, or some flattened biscuit tins nailed together, or, if they were lucky, the shelter of one brick wall. That inexpressible, dogged readiness to endure anything had already gripped the camp. They had a leader, Dhlamini. They would see it through.

When I got to Pretoria, accompanied by a friend of mine in the High Commissioner's Office, I was granted an interview with the Chief Secretary.

"This afternoon," he told me, "the Union Native Affairs Department asked us—the Basutoland Government—to deport the leaders of the gang. We told them, 'Nothing doing.' If they want to deal with criminals on their own territory it is for them to make the first move, not us."

For several weeks, apparently, the South African Government had been trying to persuade the High Commissioner to take action, a clear indication that they knew very well where the criminals were and who they were. Quite rightly, Basutoland had refused to get involved in what was, after all, a domestic affair and the concern of the Union. Relationships were sufficiently strained between the two governments in any case, and it would have been quite possible for the Union to accuse Basutoland of "interference." She had done it before, over other issues, at the U.N. and elsewhere.

In the meanwhile, the squatter camp grew. The City Council decided to apply for an eviction order under the Prevention of Illegal Squatting Act. This would have had the effect of leaving gangsters in possession and depriving the squatters of any hope of return to their homes. It was a fantastically unjust decision, and I decided to fight it—to fight it even though it meant that the squatter camp, with all the inevitable hardships it must entail, would remain and would grow. It was a difficult decision to make, and we had very little time to organise. The application to the magistrate was due to be heard on the following morning, and when I arrived at the camp at eight-thirty in the morning I found Dhlamini standing, weary after a night of watching, outside one of the hessian shelters.

"Have you got a lawyer?"

"I have got a lawyer—Mr. Lowenberg."

"Have you told him about the meeting this morning?"

Dhlamini looked at me in perplexity. It was impossible to explain the intricacies of legal proceedings to him when he had so heavy a burden to carry. He must have felt like

Moses on the first day of the Exodus. His people were behind him, but they were weary and they had little to look forward to save discomfort and more weariness.

I rang up Lowenberg, explained the situation as fully as I could, then made a dash for the Magistrates' Court, where the hearing was already in progress. I was fifteen minutes late, and Lowenberg was nowhere to be seen. It looked as though the eviction would go by default. There was no doubt that both the police and the City Council could put up a strong case. I was told I had no legal standing and could say nothing. The minutes ticked by. Still no Lowenberg. I was getting desperate, when at last the door opened and he came in—with a brief-case but, as I well knew, with no brief. He managed to persuade the magistrate that an adjournment was necessary, as he had not been able to collect all the evidence he needed. He did the same thing again when the hearing reassembled in the afternoon. We had a whole long weekend in which to prepare our case. It was just sufficient.

On the following Tuesday the magistrate granted what was in fact to be a six months' reprieve, a six months' period in which the local authority must try to persuade the government to take action against the "Russian" leaders and restore law and order in Newclare and the squatters to their homes.

In the meanwhile the African National Congress began to collect evidence from the people who had been driven out of Newclare South. Cases were prepared. The police were given chapter and verse for incident after incident. I myself checked up on the facts by visiting the "Russian" zone and seeing the houses and the rooms left empty by the squatters, some of them still empty, most occupied by the gangsters. The authorities took no action. Newclare,

in effect, became organised into two armed camps, with a
bridge in between which was the scene of fighting over the
weekends. The Civil Guard operated round the squares
where the squatters were; Dhlamini set up a "headquarters"; over two thousand people began a new and bitter
life, as the winds whistled through their pathetic cardboard walls and the shacks jostled one another for a yard
or two of space. In the meanwhile the authorities argued.
The "Russians" stayed. The children began to get sick.

Quite close to Reno Square our mission had built a small
nursery school, and we decided that we should use it at
night for the squatters' children, to try to save them from
the worst of the winter cold. I appealed for blankets and
for the money to buy warm clothes. The press supported
my appeals, and night after night in the *Star* we were able
to focus attention on the camp. During the whole six
months I collected little more than three hundred pounds.

It was whilst the squatter camp in Newclare existed in
its misery that the tornado hit Albertynville. As I have
written elsewhere, within three days thousands of pounds
of clothing and food were contributed. I have always felt
that this was an interesting comment on the conscience of
white Johannesburg. Stirred to immediate and most generous action by a tornado, it could remain utterly impervi-
ous to what was happening day after day to hundreds of
its own African citizens in its midst. It was not that Johannesburg did not *know* of the Newclare tragedy; it was that
by some strange deadening of sensitiveness, some blurring
and blinding of insight, Johannesburg did not care. Or was
it really, as it is with each one of us, that it is sometimes
easier to be deaf to the voice of conscience altogether than
to allow even the whisper of its breath to reach one's ears?

However it was, the camp remained and spread. Reno

Square was as densely populated as any area in the world; two thousand people lived on a football field. From the shacks men went off to their work each day. The women could not leave their homes for fear of losing their possessions; there was no security and no privacy of any sort. One would stoop down under the low flap of tarpaulin which served as a door. When one's eyes got used to the sudden gloom, a double bed, an open brazier, a pile of blankets, a gramophone, an old and battered trunk would come into gradual focus. And, cooking over the fire or stretched on the bed, there would be the mother of the family and two or three children with her. Even in the nightmare conditions which the days and nights of winter made so desperate, there was a real though pathetic attempt at order and cleanliness. But the danger of an epidemic was real, and indeed it was a constant fight to keep the babies from gastroenteritis and the like.

The legal battles dragged on. I spent a good deal of time trying to organise what comfort and shelter I could at the nursery school. Some European women volunteered to help in preparing meals for the children. Our African caretaker and his wife gave all their time to the task. I used to spend my evenings bathing the small ones and wrapping them up in their warm blankets. It was a wonderful experience—the gradual unfolding of confidence and trust which it produced, the sense of being expected each evening at bedtime, the grubby hands thrust into mine, and the noisy chatter and laughter. I shall never forget the nights at Newclare; they have left a mark upon me which I treasure and shall treasure always.

Perhaps I can best express what I mean by describing one small incident, one amongst many, and that not particularly exciting or wonderful except in South Africa. I had been putting the younger boys to bed—about fifty of them—on the floor, rolled up in blankets. By way of custom we always knelt and said a prayer together—the *Rara oa rona* (Our Father) and Hail Mary at least. Then I visited each one before putting out the light. As I was passing Jacob's blanket he suddenly flung it off him and knelt up, a little naked figure with sparkling eyes, and pulled my hand down to his lips and kissed it. Then, without a word, he curled up in his blanket and fell asleep. It sounds so tame, telling it now. And to those who read this book and who have not known South Africa, perhaps it sounds pointless or merely sentimental. I do not know. All I know is that, in a land where every plan, every policy, every movement is directed towards separation between black and white, a moment like that is as rare and as unreal as faëry.

Indeed, looking back over the past twelve years, I think the truth which has come home to me more forcibly than any other is that of the appalling loss which white South Africa suffers without knowing it, without believing that it is a loss at all. "'Tis ye, 'tis your estrangèd faces that miss the many-splendoured thing . . ." "The many splendoured thing" of a human relationship which is disregarded, disapproved of, and discarded every day. Coming back home from the city to Sophiatown of an evening and being sure of a greeting, not from one but from half a dozen people; children smiling and running to the car with "Morning, Father," at all hours of the day or night; a warmth and a friendliness about you because you belonged—these are the intangible things that are known only to us who have lived in places like Sophiatown. Or, again, in Johannesburg itself, being certain on any day, somewhere or other, to meet friends: an errand-boy who this morning served your Mass, a messenger in one of the offices who is on the Church Council, or just one of your own flock about his business. Strange indeed that such chance encounters should warm the heart! I cannot imagine that in a London street one would have that feeling. It is because in Johannesburg the white and the black worlds which jostle one another on the same pavement are yet farther apart than the stars themselves. And present policies only make explicit, only harden this evil division between man and man, make it more impossible for friendship to grow or even to be seen as desirable in any form at all.

The loss is so great that it is inexpressible. For the Christian it ought to be so great as to be intolerable. But it is not. The Christian drawing rooms at Parktown or Houghton would, for the most part, shudder at the idea of friendship and affection existing between persons of different colours. Miscegenation, that fearful spectre which hovers over all South African society, is certainly regarded as a sin more mortal than any in the handbook of moral theology. "Am I my brother's keeper?" is a question which must for ever take second place to "Would you like your sister to marry a black man?" The great commandment, "Thou shalt love thy neighbour as thyself," cannot be applied too literally; it might endanger the close and cabined security of European Christian homes.

To keep up the barriers: that is the first essential of good government in South Africa, and it is because the Nationalists are so much more efficient and farsighted in doing so than their opponents that they increase their majority at each election. We do not care that we lose something splendid and enriching by *apartheid;* we do not even know of its existence—for we think we can do our duty to the black man without loving him; we are sure we know him better than anyone else, without knowing him as a person at all; we prefer to live in our own world and to call it Christian, if the alternative is to live in a world which is shared, culturally, spiritually, and socially with our African brethren. The kiss of Jacob still lingers, not only in my memory but in my heart and will. It is a symbol of something so precious that I believe I would spend my whole life and all my strength striving to make it real to white South Africa. I am sure I should not succeed. You cannot, even in a lifetime, open the eyes of the blind or unstop the ears of the deaf. That is the prerogative of God himself.

So the squatters in Newclare settled down and waited. Somehow, somewhere, their case would be argued and justice would be done and they could go home. The winter gave place to the short, bright African spring, which is a hardly noticeable transition to summer; not noticeable at all in Newclare, where there are so few growing things except the grass. But with the summer, although there was relief from the bitter nights and the dust-laden winds, came the rain. The rain and the flies. The camp began to stink. The flimsy shacks were sodden; so were the beds and blankets beneath that leaking tarpaulin or that badly jointed iron. I begged for roofing material and got a hundred pounds' worth from a friend whose brother owned a building yard. It was just rolls of thick damp-course material, but at least it kept the worst of the rain off.

Soon Reno Square was so crowded that no more families could possibly edge in, and the camp overflowed on to the Charles Phillips Square. It was a bit more orderly there; there was more room, and the shacks tended to be built of wooden packing cases rather than hessian or tin. There was, in fact, a dangerous air of permanence about the place which made the authorities hasten their deliberations and which finally induced the City Council to press again for an eviction order. The Medical Officer of Health had every reason to fear for the health of the people. The old slogan, "Disease knows no colour bar," began to work.

In spite of our efforts (including deputations to the minister from the Council) to compel action against the gangsters, the government, the police, and the European public of the city refused to bestir themselves. It became clear before the end of the year that the squatters would have to face a definite and final demand for eviction. From the point of view of their own health and well-being almost anything would be better than that sodden, muddy patch of ground with its mass of pitiful shelters. "Bundles of derelict humanity . . ." they were called by one of the newspapers; it was an apt description. Nevertheless, their compulsory eviction would be a triumph for lawlessness and at the same time a fearful indictment of the authorities who, knowing full well where the crime lay, did nothing to bring it home to the criminals.

I was convinced at the time, and I am still convinced today, that this inertia was deliberate and calculated. The Western Areas Removal Scheme, involving the expropriation of all non-Europeans from Sophiatown, Martindale, and Newclare, was crystallising into its final shape. Unrest and tension, therefore, were most valuable and potent propaganda weapons for the government. It would be a grave mistake to ensure peace and justice for the Newclare squatters if it meant, in any kind of way, the condonation of their existence as legitimate citizens in that area. No better explanation of the official attitude has yet been put forward, anyhow, and I am quite ready to believe that there is none. The most that we could do was to ensure that the eviction should take place not to some far-off country area like Hammanskraal, but to an existing urban location, Moroka. On the eve of the eviction I wrote an article for the Johannesburg *Star* and said:

> The squatters' camp and the "Russians" are just pathetic symptoms—devil's sacraments—of despair. They say unmistakably, "Here is an area where no permanence, no security can be expected. Let us demonstrate our recognition of the fact that we are just flotsam and jetsam—that here we have no abiding place." So, at dawn, the lorries arrive—people, human beings, are crowded into them with what few possessions they have rescued. The trek to Moroka begins, to bare veldt beneath a winter sky, to the building again of something which can be called a home. Doubly "displaced persons" leave to their enemies the places they have known and the flimsy shelters they have set up. Where will it end? Who cares? Yet these are men and women, made in the image and likeness of God. Can we, European representatives of a Christian civilisation, sleep easily in our beds? It is God whom we insult by our apathy and it is to Him ultimately that we must make answer.

My question—rhetorical, perhaps, but intended at least to compel some attention—went unheeded and unanswered. The Europeans I had addressed in my article did not find it hard to sleep. I did not really expect that they would.

I was there on the morning the lorries arrived and watched the shacks being dismantled and their inhabitants salvaging what they could take with them. I was there at Moroka and saw the empty plots, twenty feet by twenty feet square, on which the squatters were dumped. I was there a few days later to watch the new shacks rising from the new mud, to try to help with a bit more roofing material or a few blankets.

Dhlamini was disconsolate and helpless in this new and vast "temporary camp," where sixty thousand others from the previous squatter movements at Orlando had for four or five years already been living and who now resented the intrusion of newcomers. There was no way, either, of holding them together, for their sites were carefully spaced in between existing shacks and houses. It was a defeat, and Dhlamini knew it. From time to time he came to see me to tell me of some problem or other. He had lost his job; the "Russians" had friends at Moroka who made life difficult for him and his friends; the children had all lost their places in school, for they could not travel every day back to Newclare, and the Moroka schools were full twice over. "Can the Father come and meet the people? The people are suffering too much, too much, Father. Can the Father see the superintendent? The superintendent threatens us that we must not stay together, we must go out in one month. Father, where can we go? Where can we go?"

I have told the story of the Newclare squatter movement not only because I know every smallest detail of it but because I think it illustrates better than most events the kind of thing I have tried to fight against over the years. It shows, in the helplessness and suffering of a whole section of the urban African community, not only the consequences of European apathy and unconcern but the logical and inevitable result of an *apartheid* policy. For if you really believe in *apartheid* as Dr. Verwoerd believes in it, if you really believe in white supremacy as Mr. Strijdom believes in it—then you are not concerned with persons as persons, and you cease to be concerned with justice as justice. These things become secondary. Persons become

114

pawns in a political manoeuvre, and justice becomes a ludicrous parody of all that civilised countries understand by the term. Yet whenever I pass Reno Square today I feel a lifting of my heart. Is it because I saw there so much human courage and gaiety in the midst of so much degradation? Or is it, perhaps, because a little African boy leapt from his blankets and kissed my hand?

VII. Sophiatown

SOPHIATOWN! How hard it is to capture and to convey the
magic of that name! Once it is a matter of putting pen to
paper, all the life and colour seem to leave it; and failing
to explain its mysterious fascination is somehow a betrayal
of one's love for the place. It is particularly important to
me to try to paint the picture that I know and that is yet
so elusive, for in a few years Sophiatown will cease to exist.
It will be, first of all, a rubble heap, destruction spreading
like some contagion through the streets (it has begun already), laying low the houses, good and bad alike, that
I have known; emptying them of the life, the laughter, and
the tears of the children—till the place is a grey ruin lying
in the sun. Then, I suppose, the factories will begin to go
up, gaunt impersonal blocks of cement, characterless and
chill, however bright the day. And in a few years men will
have forgotten that this was a living community and a very
unusual one. It will have slipped away into history, and
that a fragmentary history of a fraction of time. Perhaps
it will awaken faint echoes in the memory of some who
recall that it was to Sophiatown that Kumalo came seeking Absalom, his son. But they will never remember what
I remember of it; and I cannot put my memories on paper,
or, if I do, they will only be like the butterflies pinned,
dead and lustreless, on the collector's board. Nevertheless,
I must try.

Sophiatown! The name has about it a certain historical and almost theological sound. It recalls Sancta Sophia, Holy Wisdom, and the dreaming city where her temple is built. I have never heard of another Sophiatown in the world, though I suppose there must be one; it is such a euphonious name, for one thing. And, of course, it has a history and a meaning as romantic in its way as anything connected with the Eastern Mediterranean. As romantic but also about as different as it could well be.

Some fifty years ago, when Johannesburg was still a mining dorp, a planned and growing town yet small and restricted in area, a certain Mr. Tobiansky dreamed of a European suburb in the west, on the rocky outcrop which is shadowed by the spur known as Northcliff. It is quite a long way from the centre of town, about four and a half miles in fact, but not an impossible distance. It was a most attractive site in every way, for it had "features": it was not like the flat and uninteresting central area of the city. It could hold its own in natural beauty with Parktown and Houghton, soon to become the most fashionable suburbs, and, like them, it had iron-red rock for a foundation and for a problem in civil engineering.

Mr. Tobiansky bought a large plot of ground and named it in gratitude and admiration after his wife, Sophia. As he pegged out the streets he named many of them after his children: Edith and Gerty and Bertha and Toby and Sol. So from the very beginning Sophiatown had a homely and "family" feel about it. There was nothing "upstage" or snobbish about those names, just as there was nothing pretentious about the kind of houses which began to spring up. In fact, there was nothing very planned about it either. Still the veldt and the rock were more noticeable than the houses: the streets ran up and down the *kopje* and stopped short when the *kopje* became too steep. There was on one side a wide sweep of what you might call meadowland: an empty plot of ground which provided clay for the bricks and a good playing field for the children.

There seemed to be no reason on earth why Sophiatown should not be as popular a suburb as Parktown itself, perhaps even more popular because it was more open, higher up on the six-thousand-foot plateau which is Johannesburg. But Mr. Tobiansky had reckoned without the Town Council; or perhaps already that mischievous and unpredictable voice had whispered something about the future. Whatever it was, the Council decided that a growing town must have sewage-disposal facilities: and it decided further that those facilities must be in the Western Area of the young Johannesburg. The natural and immediate consequence of this decision was the end of Mr. Tobiansky's dream. Sophiatown ceased to be attractive in any way to those Europeans who wished to buy land and to build homes in the suburbs. Mr. Tobiansky could not sell to white Johannesburg and for a while he could not sell to anyone else.

Then once again the Town Council intervened. The First World War brought a wave of industrialisation, and with it the need for African labour. The only existing location, Pimville, had been planned and planted some ten miles from the centre of the town. There was certainly need for another location which would house the African workers and which might be a little more conveniently sited for their work. The Western Area was once more chosen. Sewage disposal and a native location seemed to go together. The Western Native Township, with accommodation for some three thousand families, was built. A tall iron fence was erected all round it. The Africans moved in. So, some forty years ago, began the African occupation of the western suburbs.

As soon as the location was established, Tobiansky found himself in an area where the non-European was in the majority. There was nothing to prevent him selling his land to Africans, coloureds, and Asiatics. Under one of President Kruger's laws he was perfectly safeguarded for doing so, and as a good businessman he did the obvious thing. The obvious thing but not the most usual in South Africa. For when Tobiansky sold freehold properties to African purchasers, he was in fact establishing a unique situation. He was making possible an African—or at least a non-white—suburb in Johannesburg. He knew, no doubt, what he was doing. He could hardly have known the far-reaching consequences of his action. For as Johannesburg expanded, so did its need for African labour. Apart from the squalid slums of Vrededorp and the distant cor-rugated-iron location of Pimville, there was nowhere for the people to live except the Western Native Township and the suburbs of Sophiatown, Martindale, and Newclare which surrounded it. Houses sprang up in Edith Street and elsewhere: houses of all types, all sizes, all colours. They crept up towards the rocks on top of the hill; they spread out towards the brickfields. By 1920 or thereabouts it had become quite obvious that here was an area which be-longed by right of possession to the non-European half of Johannesburg. It was not so evident at that time that white suburbia was also spreading rapidly westwards and that it was becoming especially the residential area of the Eu-ropean artisan. Sophiatown had come to maturity, had a character and an atmosphere of its own, and in the suc-ceeding thirty-odd years that character and that atmos-phere deepened and became only the more permanent.

When I arrived to take over as priest-in-charge of the Anglican mission in September 1943, the place had for many years assumed the appearance it has today. It is that which I wish so greatly to put into words. Yet I know I cannot succeed.

They say that Sophiatown is a slum. Strictly in terms of the Slums Act they are absolutely correct, for the density of the population is about twice what it should be—70,000 instead of 30,000. But the word "slum" to describe Sophiatown is grossly misleading and especially to people who know the slums of Europe or the United States. It conjures up immediately a picture of tenement buildings, old and damp, with crumbling stone and dark cellars. The Dickensian descriptions come to mind, and the gloom and dreariness which he could convey so vividly are there in the imagination as soon as the word "slum" is read or recognised. In that sense Sophiatown is not and never has been a slum. There are no tenements; there is nothing really old; there are no dark cellars. Sometimes, looking up at Sophiatown from the Western Native Township across the main road, I have felt I was looking at an Italian village somewhere in Umbria. For you do "look up" at Sophiatown, and in the evening light, across the blue-grey haze of smoke from braziers and chimneys, against a saffron sky, you see close-packed, red-roofed little houses. You see on the farthest sky line the tall and shapely blue-gum trees (which might be cypresses if it were really Italy). You see, moving up and down the hilly streets, people in groups: people with colourful clothes; people who, when you come up to them, are children playing, dancing, and standing round the braziers. And above it all you see the Church of Christ the King, its tower visible north, south, east, and west, riding like a great ship at anchor upon the grey and golden waves of the town beneath. In the evening towards the early South African sunset there is very little of the slum about Sophiatown. It is a human dwelling place. It is as if old Sophia Tobiansky herself were gathering her great family about her, watching over them before they slept. Essentially Sophiatown is a gay place and, for all the occasional moments of violence and excitement, a kindly one too. But like every other place with a character, you have to live in it, to get the feel of its life, before you can really know it. And in the whole of South Africa there are only a handful of white citizens who have had that privilege.

The decision to move the Western Areas, to destroy all the properties built there, and to transplant the whole population to Meadowlands, four miles farther away from the city, was taken by people who had no firsthand knowledge of the place at all. How could they be expected to know it, when in their eyes it represents the very antithesis of a sound "native policy"? Freehold rights and permanence, the building up of a living community—these things are contrary to the whole doctrine of *apartheid*. They assume that the African has a right to live in the city as well as to work in it. Such an assumption is heresy to Dr. Verwoerd. It cannot be allowed. But what is it that makes Sophiatown so precious? Why should we care so much to preserve what, on any showing, is two thirds a slum area? I have asked myself that question a thousand times as I have walked its streets, visited its people in their homes, taken the Blessed Sacrament to the sick and dying. I have asked it when the dust was flying and the wind tossing the refuse about in those sordid and overcrowded back yards, and I have asked it when, looking for someone at night, I have stumbled in the dark across children asleep on the floor, packed tight together beneath a table to make room for others also to sleep. I have asked it when, on a blisteringly hot December day, the sun has beaten down on the iron ceiling of a shack and the heat has mercilessly pressed its substance upon that old, frail creature lying on the bed. I have asked it as I lay awake at night listening to the drunken shouts and the noisy laughter from the yard behind the mission. In other words, I know Sophiatown at its worst: in all weathers, under all conditions, as a slum living up to its reputation. I still love it and believe it has a unique value. But why?

In the first place, because it is not a "location." Part of the meaning of white South Africa's attitude to the African is revealed in that word "location." In America it generally has reference to part of the technique of the cinema industry. A film is made "on location" in order to give it the genuine flavour and atmosphere required by the story. But everywhere else in the world, so far as I know, the word just means a place, a site, a prescribed area. That is why, no doubt, it was chosen by the European when he decided that the African must have somewhere to live when he came to work in the towns and cities of his own country. He could not live in a suburb. He could not live in a village. He could not live in the residential area of the town itself. He could only work in those places. And because he is an abstraction—"a native"—he must have an abstraction for his home. A location in fact, a place to be in for so long as his presence is necessary and desirable to his European boss. A place from which to move on when it ceases to be necessary or desirable that he should stay.

The locations of South Africa for the most part live up to their name. They are abstract, colourless places. Every town has one on its outskirts. Today it is necessary by law that there should be a buffer strip at least five hundred yards wide between any location and the town it serves. There must be the same distance between a location and a main road. Nothing must be erected on the buffer strip —not even a pair of football goal posts. It must mark that tremendous and vital distinction between civilisation and barbarism upon which the doctrine of white supremacy rests. No one of either race may linger on that strip of land, for in that way it might become a meeting place. It is, in exact and literal terms, a no man's land; and it is meant to be just that.

There is a noticeable and depressing similarity about all locations. It is not only that for the most part the houses are built on mass-production lines and at the lowest cost compatible with minimum housing standards. It is that at the same time they are sited in the most monotonous way imaginable, as if to say: "There must be no variety in a location. Variety is a characteristic of the human being. His home is a reflection of that characteristic. But because the African is a native, it is a quality which simply does not exist." Sometimes, with the older locations, tall iron fences were erected and give the impression not only of a kind of imprisonment but of a fortification, as though the location were totally alien to the life around it and had to be defended at all costs from any contact with it. Today the buffer strip serves the same purpose and is less expensive. So, in a location, you have row upon row of small boxlike houses of almost identical shape and size. Such variation as there is marks the end of one housing contract and the beginning of another or the start, perhaps, of some new experiment in pre-fab construction. It is never variety for its own sake. It is a location—not a village, you must remember. As such it is unnecessary for the streets to be named. You simply number the houses from one to two or ten thousand and you leave it at that. If, later on, a few streets receive baptism, it is too late for old habits to be broken. Mrs. Kambula lives at 6002A Orlando. Mrs. Marite lives "in the four thousands." It all helps to keep the idea of abstraction alive.

The great advantage of the location is that it can be controlled. People who come to visit their friends for the weekend must have permits before they can set foot upon that arid, municipal turf. It is so much easier, too, to prevent the native feeling himself a permanent resident in our cities if nonpayment of rent is a criminal offence rather than a civil one. The presence, in every location, of a European superintendent with his small army of officials, black and white, and his municipal police, is a sound and healthy reminder that in South Africa the African needs the white man to guide and direct his daily life. And in the sphere of broader strategy it is also wiser to have the native living in one large but easily recognisable camp than scattered around the town in smaller groupings. If there is trouble in Johannesburg, for instance, Orlando can be "contained" by a comparatively small force. It is not a bad target from the air either. And its buffer strip ensures that no European suburb will be hit by mistake.

In the larger locations there are shops, and they are even allowed under licence to be owned and run by Africans. All the essential services are provided, though lighting for your house is not necessarily regarded as essential. It is not untypical of the location concept that in Johannesburg the largest power station in the Southern Hemisphere stands at the gate of Orlando. It supplies electricity to the city. Orlando is lit by candles and paraffin lights. Churches, schools, and clinics exist in locations through the effort of the various missionary and voluntary organisations. Municipal social workers go about their business. Men and women live there and make their family life a reality. But always I have the feeling (and I am sure I am meant to have it, as are the inhabitants themselves) that a location cannot *belong* to anyone except the people who control it, the European officials who live far away in the city, that other abstraction, "the municipality." Always, even in considering the better aspects of location life (and there are some, I suppose), I seem to hear the voice of the Manager of Non-European Affairs saying: "We are going to do you good, whether you like it or not, for we alone know what is good for you!"

Sophiatown is not a location. That is my first reason for loving it. It is so utterly free from monotony in its siting, in its buildings, and in its people. By a historical accident it started life as a suburb, changed its colour at an early moment in its career, and then decided to go all out for variety. A £3000 building jostles a row of single rooms: an "American" barber's shop stands next door to an African herbalist's store with its dried roots and dust-laden animal hides hanging in the window. You can go into a store to buy a packet of cigarettes and be served by a Chinaman, an Indian, or a Pakistani. You can have your choice of doctors and clinics even, for they also are not municipally controlled. There are churches of every denomination and of almost every imaginable sect. There is one, for example, known as the "Donkey Church," upon whose squat, square tower there stands, in place of the traditional weathercock, an ass. I would not know its real origin, except that it is, I believe, a schism from the Methodist Church. Nor do I wish to suggest any approval for schism as such: for nothing has done so much damage to African Christianity than

126

its fissiparousness. But somehow or other that little donkey represents the freedom that has existed down the years in Sophiatown, and when I pass it I metaphorically lift my hat. It reminds me, for one thing, of the truth that G. K. Chesterton so simply and so profoundly taught in his poem:

> The tattered outlaw of the earth
> Of ancient crooked will;
> Starve, scourge, deride me: I am dumb,
> I keep my secret still.

> Fools! For I also had my hour:
> One far fierce hour and sweet:
> There was a shout about my ears,
> And palms before my feet.

Basically, white South Africa has the same benign or un-benign contempt for the African as man for the donkey. Was it not Smuts himself who said once that "the African has the patience of the ass"? And so Sophiatown is written off as a slum area; its values must be those of the slum; its people must be dirty, undesirable, and, above all, unseen. Like the donkey that stands as a symbol above their streets, they are useful for their labour, for they are strong. But, as Dr. Verwoerd says, there is no place for them above that level in society itself. "I keep my secret still. . . ." The secret of Sophiatown is not only its variety, it is its hidden heroisms, or rather its unknown heroes and heroines, its saints uncanonised and unsung. I know very many.

In the first place, let me say it frankly, any young person who keeps straight when the dice are loaded so heavily against him needs virtue of a heroic quality. The overcrowded rooms of Sophiatown, wherein whole families must sleep and must perform all their human functions as best they may, do not make morality an easy thing. The lack of opportunity for fulfilling his personality in any productive way does not make it easy, either, for a lad to escape the street-corner gang and the excitement of gambling. The endless, grey vista of an existence which is based upon poverty is not the kind of outlook which helps to keep a boy or his girl friend alive to ultimate standards of beauty, truth, and goodness.

Again and again, hearing confessions, I have asked myself how I could advise these children, how warn them, how comfort them when they have fallen. ". . . I have sinned exceedingly in thought, word, and deed, by my fault, my own fault, my own most grievous fault. . . ." Have you *really*? No doubt the actual sin is grave enough —fornication or stealing or fighting—but what would I have done in your place? And whose fault is it in the sight of God? And what, anyway, can I advise?

"Don't let yourself get into bad company. . . . Don't be idle. . . . Find some other interest than gambling. . . . Love? Well, it's not so easy to describe it . . . it must have the quality of unselfishness."

God forgive me! I find myself giving advice that, in those circumstances, I *know* I could not follow. And yet, again and again, those gentle men and women, those fresh, gay lads and girls try to follow, try desperately hard to obey it, and even in their failures do not make environment or circumstance an excuse. To keep your self-respect when you are *expected* to have less than your white *baas;* to keep your home neat and tidy and to dress your children in fresh clothes; to pay for their school books regularly and to see that they are fed properly. All this against a background of overcrowding, of the need to be up and away to work before you have time to eat your own breakfast or to clean the room that is your home. It needs the kind of virtue which most European Christians in South Africa have never come within a mile of. And it is common in Sophiatown. I do not refer just to our own church people, though naturally they are the ones I know best and most intimately. There is in that "black spot" (to use the minister's offensive title) a great well of courage and cheerfulness in face of adversity which has been through the years an inspiration and a challenge to at least one Christian priest. I can shut my eyes for a moment and see old blind Margaret tapping her way along the street in the darkness which has been hers for many long years. Always, half an hour before the early Mass, she will be there in church, prostrate in prayer. Day by day I will find her spending an hour or more before the statue of Our Lady which she has never seen, and if I stop her in the street I will be greeted with that wonderful smile and the lifting of her sightless eyes to my face. . . .

Or, after Mass on Sunday morning, there will be old Tryphena Mtembu. She has spent all her years (at least all those that I have known) mending sacks and inhaling cement dust into her old lungs, so that she is never free from a fierce cough. She lives in a single dark room and "does" for herself, although a few years ago she fell and broke her leg and has to fight her way on to the early-morning bus with a crutch in one gnarled and work-lined hand. Tryphena has a wonderful flow of language, and her epithets are not always what you might expect from a devout and faithful old lady. She is, in fact, very much a product of the Old Kent Road, and were it not for her broken leg I believe she would sing and dance to "Knees up, Mother Brown" with the best of them. I also believe that her place in heaven is assured. For how could it be otherwise with one who fronts adversity with those twinkling and mischievous brown eyes and defies poverty to get her down with that marvellous and undaunted faith?

Or, again, there is Piet, who put all his money into the house in Millar Street, where he now sits, crippled with arthritis, and hoping to die before they come and demolish his home over his head. Old Piet, our churchwarden for so long, who worked for over thirty years in one of the best furniture shops in the city and was rewarded by his employers with a pittance which would not keep him alive. Never have I heard him complain, even when it was obvious that the handling of great bales of material was too much for him in his old age, even when it was a painful and weary journey for him to climb the short hill to the church he loved.

It would be easy but not very interesting, I suppose, to list a score of others of all ages and types who have lived in Sophiatown for the better part of their lives and who by their very living have enriched and beautified it greatly. A priest can see these things. Sometimes he cannot find words in which to express them. But Johannesburg knows nothing of them and can know nothing, for it does not care. To Johannesburg, Sophiatown is a slum: a native slum at that. How could it possibly have any human dignity about it?

But there is one feature of life in Sophiatown which everyone can recognise—everyone who goes there, that is. It is inescapable from the first moment when you step out of your car or stop to ask the way from the tram stop to the mission. It does not matter much what time of day it is either. Nor does it make a great deal of difference who you are or what your business—provided you are not a policeman in uniform. It is the children.

I remember the first day of my arrival there on a September morning twelve years ago. After breakfast at the mission I was told, "There's a school Mass on in the church. They'd like to see you. Will you come across?" The church is a large one by any standards. As I stood at the back and looked towards the High Altar I could see nothing but row upon row of black, curly heads. It seemed impossible to imagine that there could be quite so many children—impossible, anyhow, to imagine myself getting to know even a fraction of them. But I was wrong on both counts. This congregation represented only about half the children in one school. Soon, within a few weeks, I was beginning not only to know them but to compare them mentally with other children I had known in England. I found that I quite easily thought of their names, their features, and their characters in the same terms as of those who were already part of my family, part of my very life. And the reason was not hard to discover.

The Sophiatown child is the friendliest creature on earth and the most trusting. God knows why it should be so, but it is. You will be walking across the playground and suddenly feel a tug at your sleeve or a pressure against your knee; and then there will be a sticky hand in yours. "Hallo, Farther, hallo, Seester, how are you? Hallo, hallo, hallo. . . ." You will come back from Johannesburg, as I have done a thousand times, fed up and sick with weariness from that soulless city, and immediately you are caught in a rush and scurry of feet, in faces pressed against your car window, in arms stretching up to reach yours whether you like it or not. You are *home*. Your children are around you—ten of them, a hundred, a thousand; you belong to them and they will never let you forget it. How, then, can you fail to love the place where such things happen? Its dusty, dirty streets and its slovenly shops, its sprawling and unplanned stretches of corrugated-iron roof: its fetid and insanitary yards? ". . . and the streets of the city shall be full of boys and girls playing in the streets thereof . . ." is a description of the heavenly Jerusalem. It is a good one. And anyone who has lived as I have in that "slum" called Sophiatown will recognise how swiftly, through the presence of its children and through their unspoilt and unassailable laughter, heaven can break in upon this old and dreary world.

I have said that Sophiatown is a gay place. It is more. It has a vitality and an exuberance about it which belong to no other suburb in South Africa, certainly to no white suburb. It positively sparkles with life. Sometimes when I have been depressed by the apparent success of the present government in selling the idea of "white supremacy," I have pulled myself up by thinking just for a moment or two of the African people as I know them in Sophiatown. There is something so robust and strong about their way of dealing with each frustration, which is each day, that it is even laughable to think that such an idea can endure. And in fact it is by laughter, so often, that the problems and the sorrows are fronted and overcome. It is by that magnificent sense of humour and by the fitness with which it is expressed that victory is won in the daily struggle and will ultimately be won in the struggle for true nationhood.

A good example of the kind of humour I have known and loved is to be seen in Sophiatown any weekend, when the "Sophiatown Scottish" are on the march. In the distance, on a Sunday afternoon, you will hear the beating of a drum and the sound of a far trumpet. Soon, at the farthest end of Victoria Road, you will see a small crowd moving towards you and becoming a large crowd as it moves. Then, if you are wise, you will wait, and witness the unique and heartening sight of an all-African, all-female band dressed in tartan kilts, white gloves, bandsman's staff, and accoutrement, swinging down the road with marvellous gusto. Behind them will come the spectators, not marching in step but dancing with complete abandon and, surrounding them as always when there's a sight, a crowd of the children, dancing, too, and singing as they dance. Somehow the "Sophiatown Scottish" stand for so much more than a happy Sunday afternoon. They stand for the joy and gaiety which is *there*, deep in the heart of the African and ready to break out in one form or another whenever and wherever he is at home.

Another example of the same thing I have seen very often at political meetings, especially when European police are present to take names and to record speeches. What could so easily, in other circumstances, become a dangerously tense situation through the provocative and contemptuous attitude of the authorities becomes a ridiculous and irrelevant matter. "After all," the Africans seem to say, "this is only an incident, and a minor one, in our progress to freedom and to fulfilment. Why not laugh at it, shrug it off with a song?" And so they do.

Sophiatown! It is not your physical beauty which makes you so lovable; not that soft line of colour which sometimes seems to strike across the greyness of your streets; not the splendour of the evening sky which turns your drabness into gold—it is none of these things. It is your people. Yet somehow I do not think it can be the same when you yourself have been destroyed and your houses are just rubble and the factories begin to go up and to smother you with their bulk and size. Even though your people will still be here in Johannesburg, in the wide symmetry of some location such as Meadowlands, there will have been a loss immeasurable. The truth is that Sophiatown is a community, a living organism which has grown up through the years and which has struck its roots deep in this particular place and in this special soil. So have I known it to be. A community with all the ordinary problems of a community and made up of people and families both bad and good. A community, not an abstraction, and therefore *personal* and real in all its aspects. And because it is an African community, living in a city of South Africa, it has to grow together in a unique way. Xosa and Mosotho, Shangaan and Motswana, Indian and Chinese, coloured and white have all contributed something to it. And in my opinion they have all had something of value to contribute. The place is cosmopolitan in a real sense and has about it that atmosphere which belongs to cosmopolitan towns the world over. It is, in that sense, unique. The most unlikely and unexpected things can happen there and not appear at all unlikely or seem incongruous. So you have to be prepared, if you live in the midst of it as a priest, for every conceivable problem at every hour of the day or night. How, then, can you fail to love it?

A great deal is said by sociologists and others of "the breakdown of tribal custom" and "the disastrous impact of Western industrialism upon the urban African." That sentence itself is stiff with the jargon of the race-relations textbook. But when you live in Sophiatown you don't see it that way at all. You see Mrs. X., who has a drunken husband and five children to support—and what must she do? You see Mr. Y., whose wife left him two years ago and the kids are growing up; what is he to plan for them, can the

"Father" help him? You see young Joel, who has just left
school and got a "tea-boy" job in the city, but he longs to
do his Matric. and can't find the time or the money or the
quietness for work that he needs. You are called to that
room in Tucker Street, where Joseph is fighting for his life
against advanced t.b., and in spite of all your efforts you
can't get a bed anywhere and you wonder—well, you wonder what it all means within the Providence of God. And
you hear that Jane has got into trouble and the boy won't
admit his fault; and you run *posthaste* to see her father
before he goes out with a sjambok. . . . And then there's
George, arrested for carrying *dagga,* and there's Michael,
whom you've not seen for weeks, but you hear he's drink-
ing. . . . But behind them all, behind the "problems"
which come the way of every priest in every parish in
Christendom, there is that great mass of folk who live ordinary lives in extraordinary conditions and who *are* the
Christian community in Sophiatown. And a more vital
Christian community it would be hard to find anywhere.

I wonder, for instance, how many parishes in England
today would have a Mass in the dark of a winter morning
at half-past five and get a congregation of twenty or thirty
people? And that not just once, but week after week? I
wonder how many churches today are full on Sunday
morning at six o'clock and again at eleven? Yet this is but
the outward form of something far deeper and more profound. It is in fact the answer to the sociologist's question
—at least it is part of the answer. The only thing which
is meeting the need for a sense of "community," of "belonging," in the broken and shattered tribalism of the
town-dwelling African is the Church. It is for that reason
that these present years of crisis are of such tremendous
significance. If the Church fails in bearing her witness on

the colour question *now,* she will never, in my opinion, have a second opportunity. Here in Sophiatown over the past thirty years and more we have been engaged in building a Christian community. It is that community which is now being smashed to pieces in the interests of a racial ideology. And as we watch our people's homes being reduced to heaps of rubble we watch also the destruction of something which cannot be built again so easily or so fair. When Sophiatown is finally obliterated and its people scattered, I believe that South Africa will have lost not only a place but an ideal.

Day that I have loved, day that I have loved,
The night is here. . . .

VIII. Who Goes There?

IN A WORLD which has grown painfully familiar with the idea of restrictions upon personal freedom and with jargon about the "Iron Curtain," it is more than necessary to ask exactly what we are prepared to do about it. Whether as Christians, who claim that the sacredness of personality is inviolable, or as citizens of a commonwealth which boasts its regard for freedom, there are certain challenging facts which we cannot avoid. At least we cannot avoid them if we are honest. As I write these words, for instance, there are fifty-seven South African citizens who in one year have been refused passports. One of them, Mrs. Jessie Mc-Pherson, happens to be chairman of the South African Labour Party. It is freely stated (and indeed the courts have themselves upheld the contention) that a passport is a privilege and not a right. But the effect of the latest legislation (the Passport Regulation Act of 1955) is to make it impossible for any citizen of South Africa to move out of the country without a passport or a travel permit issued by the state. In other words, the government can and does refuse the "privilege" of freedom of movement to any citizen who, for one reason or another, has incurred its displeasure. The Commonwealth has an "Iron Curtain" every bit as formidable (and in some respects perhaps more so) as that across eastern Europe. So it is rather important to examine the situation carefully. What, in fact, is happening to freedom of movement in South Africa? Does it still exist?

Let me begin by telling the story of Oliver Tambo, at present one of the few African attorneys in the country and acting secretary of the African National Congress. Oliver was born about forty years ago in a little village called Bizana in eastern Pondoland, deep in the heart of the Transkeian Native Reserve. Both his parents were heathen and illiterate; his father was fairly wealthy and according to custom had several wives. Oliver was, in fact, the second child of the third wife. This is significant to the story, for it is so often said, and I suppose believed, that the African cannot possibly make the jump from primitive to Western society in such a short span as a hundred or two hundred years. Indeed, Dr. Verwoerd believes that he cannot make it at all and that in fact tribalism is more important to African development than the Christian ethic. Oliver sat on the *stoep* of our library a few days ago telling me his story, and as he spoke the sunlight fell upon and accentuated the marks of the knife upon his face, the marks of tribalism. It also fell upon the furrows across his forehead and at the corners of those bright, intelligent, and alert eyes of his and showed up the suffering and the sorrow that are in his face today. I have known Oliver for several years, and I have known him well in these last days when we have worked most closely together over the Bantu Education Act and the Western Areas Removal Scheme. This was the first time I had asked him about his childhood and his past.

"I went to a mission primary school," he said, "but when I got to Standard Four I began to play truant. School was boring to me, and I just stopped going. By that time my father was getting old and he had lost all his wealth; he

was a farmer, and he was just unfortunate. We were terribly poor. I thought of going out to work. It was at that
moment in my life that the first great change and chance
occurred." As he told it me, Oliver did not attempt to add
anything to the bare and simple facts. There was a famous
Anglican mission station a few miles away at Holy Cross.
One day one of the priests visited Bizana, saw Oliver's
father, who by this time had become a Christian, and
suggested taking the boy back with him to the boarding
school at the mission. It was a great opportunity, and the
old man swiftly assented.

"I arrived there," said Oliver, "on Easter Day, with one
of my stepbrothers, and I shall never forget that moment.
We entered the great church whilst the Mass of Easter was
being sung. I can still see the red cassocks of the servers,
the grey smoke of the incense, the vestments of the priest
at the altar. . . . It was a new world." The old longing for
education stirred again in the heart of that small African
boy. He worked hard, passed his standards, and found himself in the top form—and the highest that he could reach
in Holy Cross Mission.

Once again it seemed like the end: the vanishing of a
dream. There was no money at home and no chance of
getting any rich relations to help. Oliver braced himself to
face the road which so many of his people trod, the road
of labour without hope of fulfilment. But again Providence
intervened, this time in the person of Father Leary, a well-
known missionary in Pondoland. He suggested that Oliver
should go to St. Peter's School in Johannesburg, which had
then just begun its secondary course. He did more: for he
found the money. So, at sixteen, a small and bewildered
boy from the rolling lands of the Transkei found himself
for the first time in Johannesburg, in "Goli," the fabulous

city, where there was so much wealth and so much wickedness too; where in contrast to the quiet and gentle villages that Oliver had known there was the noise and clamour and rush of a town built on and built for gold. Here, if ever, was a test of adaptability. In his person there met all that could be best described as tribalism, all that could be expressed in industrialised Western society.

"I came with Robert Sonquishe, now a priest, and we went through St. Peter's together." "Went through" is a good description. Oliver got a first-class Matric. (the same examination as that taken by European school children) and a Bunga scholarship to Fort Hare, the African university college. He took his B.Sc. degree in 1941 and then began studying for his education diploma with a view to teaching.

Once more things went badly wrong. "Within two months of my final exam there was a dispute in the college with the authorities. As secretary of the Students' Representative Council I had to take the responsibility for stating the students' case. It was a small matter concerning the playing of games on Sundays, but certain principles were involved and, anyway, I had to put the case." For some reason now lost in the past, the authorities insisted on a written pledge from the students concerning their conduct but also concerning their spiritual life and their religious duties. "I asked the warden for time to pray about this, and I went to the chapel for half an hour. I *knew* I could not sign that pledge. It demanded something from me that I could not give. It would have killed my religion stone dead—an agreement with God, written and signed? I could not do it!" Oliver told the warden of his decision and was immediately expelled. His expulsion meant, so far as he could see, the end of his ambitions, for he would never get a teaching post without the diploma and with his record of expulsion for indiscipline. "I wandered into Alice" (the town nearest to Fort Hare) "and stayed there till nightfall. I just did not see what I could do. I decided, anyhow, to go back to the chapel and pray. So at eleven o'clock that night I opened the door. It was completely dark, completely empty, absolutely silent. But at the far end, near the Blessed Sacrament, there was a glow of light from the lamp which always burned there. I took that as a sign. That somewhere, however dark, there is a light. . . ."

After much anxiety and after deciding to go to Durban and work in a kitchen, at the twenty-third hour Oliver heard from St. Peter's School that there was an unexpected vacancy for a science master. So he found himself at home again in the school he loved best.

After a few years of teaching he decided to try his hand at law, studied in his spare time, took his attorney's admission, and after three more years qualified as an attorney.

I have told this story in some detail and at some length, for it shows not only the quality of the man but the quality of the struggle which faces all young Africans with ability and ambition. It all shows, I think, the quality of faith, the Christian motive at its best. Indeed, it would be hard to find a more devoted churchman than Oliver Tambo.

It was for this reason that when I heard that he had been banned in terms of the Suppression of Communism Act I took up my pen and wrote for the London *Observer* an article entitled "The Church Sleeps On." It seemed to me then and it seems to me now quite intolerable that the great mass of Christian people in South Africa should remain entirely unmoved when a man of Oliver's stature was victimised in this way. Of course it had already happened to many others, to trade unionists, to left-wing publicists, to almost every African and Indian leader of any stature. But here was, it seemed to me, a unique opportunity for the Church to protest and to demand to be heard on behalf of one of her most faithful sons. She did nothing.

The ban, in Oliver's case, restricted him to the Johannesburg municipal area and to Benoni, his place of residence. It meant that as a busy and popular lawyer he could not reach his own clients unless they happened to live in the city. It meant, further, that he could not attend any meetings or be present at any gatherings, even of a social nature. It so happened that on the occasion of Speech Day at St. Peter's School he had been invited, as a distinguished old boy, to speak. He could not risk that, but he did come to listen, hidden away from the main hall. Halfway through the afternoon, as we were moving out from one place to another, one of the boys reported to me that the Special Branch of the C.I.D. had also been listening to the speeches. Oliver had slipped away by a side entrance. The police were watching his car and he dared not go near it.

On another occasion, very recently, I rang up and asked him to supper. He was followed by the police from the moment he left his office. On yet another occasion he was urgently summoned by his family to the Transkei, and he used his telephone to send a telegram announcing the time of his arrival. In the wilds of Pondoland as he drew near his home he was stopped by a police car and questioned. He lives, in fact, always under the shadow of arrest, always watched and spied upon, always in danger of losing the tenuous liberty that remains to him. Why? Because in South Africa today the state has assumed the right to restrict absolutely the liberty of its subjects, and if they are Africans who show any powers of leadership, that restriction is justified by the single word "Communist."

The Church sleeps on. "White" Christianity is more concerned to retain its character as a law-abiding force than to express its abhorrence of such attacks on personal liberties. In spite of constant synodical resolutions and episcopal pronouncements, the Church as a whole does not care. "If one member suffer, all the members suffer with it," says St. Paul. We have travelled a very long way from that conception in Christian South Africa. It is easier to condemn communism than to practise the faith you profess. Oliver Tambo can live his hunted life and I can forget that he also belongs to the Divine Society, to the Family of God, to the Body of Christ. I can forget it because for so long in South Africa I have forgotten that man is made in the Image and Likeness of God even when he is black.

One of the phrases which recur with sickening familiarity in South Africa is "protest meeting." Looking back over the years, I can picture a great many meetings in which I have taken part. As each year has brought some new restrictive law, so a group, either created for the purpose or already existing, has rallied its followers to protest. The Suppression of Communism Act, the Citizenship Act, the Criminal Law Amendment Act—to name some at random —have all stimulated opposition in this form. Standing on the steps of the Johannesburg City Hall, or in Church Square, Pretoria, we have addressed the people. For a few days both before and after such meetings there has been some interest in the press, but in no case that I can remember has there been any real effect upon the government's attitude. It takes a great deal more than a protest meeting to impress a party which knows that on the basic issue confronting the country it can count on an almost total white unity. All that one can hope to do by public protest is to clear one's own conscience and to try at least to stir the consciences of others.

But there is one meeting of this kind which I feel to be significant in a different way. It took place very recently in Alexandra Township and I was asked to speak. It had to be on a Sunday morning, as nearly all African meetings have to be so planned, taking into account working hours, difficulties of transport, dangers of night in dark and unlit streets. Often I have found myself going straight from Mass to such a gathering; from the altar or the pulpit to the soapbox. It is a strange experience, but I believe it to be a valuable and a valid one. Anyhow, under urban African conditions it is inevitable. On this particular Sunday as I drove across the rutted roads of the township and tried to avoid the *dongas* which never get filled in, I saw on the farthest edge of Alexandra a little group of people gathering. When I got there they were already sitting in a semicircle, perhaps two hundred of them, listening quietly to an African speaker. Two police cars were drawn up on the edge of the audience; two African "specials" were sitting at the back taking down every word spoken. It was very quiet and attentive, that little gathering.

"We do not care to know," said the speaker, "what Miss Navid's politics were. We know only that she did a great work for us and our children in the three years that she was in Alexandra. Under her care Entokozweni developed wonderfully. She built a crèche for our little ones. She started vegetable clubs to help us buy food more cheaply. She began a school for those who were out of school. Now we are told she is a Communist. We do not know, we do not care about such matters. All we know is that the government has taken her away from us, has taken away our friend and will not let her work here any more. She is to be buried alive in her own country, buried alive. . . . For she cannot do the work that she is trained to do. . . ." From time to time the audience moaned and uttered that strange but expressive cry which anyone who knows Africa will remember always, "A-eee . . . a-ee!" It was indeed not unlike a funeral oration, a funeral party. What was it all about?

For the past three years and more Helen Navid, a great friend of mine, an agnostic, and one who in her student days had been attracted by Marxism, had been in charge of Entokozweni. This place, known technically as a family welfare centre, was (and is) run by a voluntary committee and aims at trying to fill some of the gaps which exist in state social welfare services in the urban areas of South Africa today. Its work is immensely varied, as varied as are the needs of the great mass of people settled in Alexandra Township itself. Anyone in charge of such a centre needs not only the technical qualifications of the social welfare worker but the qualities of patience, of compassion, and of perseverance in a high degree. Helen had all of these. She was able to build up a staff of African helpers and to earn and retain their trust. She was, in fact, employed by the government itself in a research programme concerning the incidence of cancer amongst the non-Europeans of the city. But she was also independent enough to take part in the opposition to the Western Areas Removal Scheme and the Bantu Education Act. We worked very closely together in both these battles, and never was there a more determined or efficient fighter than Helen. It was due to her hard work that committees were formed in the European suburbs of the city to serve as a platform for our speakers, a platform which was most necessary in counteracting government propaganda and most difficult to achieve. Perhaps the most successful meeting of this kind we ever had was at Parktown, a highly respectable and influential suburb, when Oliver Tambo and I spoke together, and our audience contained one or two city councillors and at least one M.P.

Helen was one of those rare people not only content to work in the background but preferring to do so. It was this quality, together with her superb efficiency and thoroughness, which made her so valubale. But neither efficiency nor unselfishness would have been sufficient of themselves without a real integrity of purpose. This she had in a high degree, and it was directed against those evil forces of repression and racialism which both of us hated so greatly, though from differing foundations of belief. And here let me say quite frankly that I have again and again found myself more able to understand and better understood amongst people of Helen Navid's quality than amongst practising Christians. That fearful barrier of respectability which so often grows up around even the most devout and devoted churchgoer is even more evident and more difficult to penetrate in South Africa, where it rests not only upon class but on colour.

I find that in writing of Helen I have written in the past tense as if she were dead. In fact, she is in Israel, and perhaps she will not return to her own country. Certainly she will not do so if it means, as the African speaker said, being "buried alive."

She was sitting in her office at Entokozweni one afternoon a few months ago when two Special Branch detectives arrived. In a sense she had been expecting them, for she knew full well that she had been under surveillance for a long time. They gave her a document and stood over her whilst she read it. It stated in effect that she must re-

sign from her present job and from all committees or societies, and it banned her from all gatherings for five years.
She was still free to work as a typist in an office or as a
factory hand or as an artist's model. She could still have a
latchkey of her own and travel on public transport and
have a cup of tea with her aunt. She was free, in fact, to do
anything except what gave life meaning: the work for
which she was trained, the fulfilment of a vocation. And,
in addition, she had allowed her South African passport to
expire and would certainly not get another. The new Passport Regulation Act would be gazetted in a week or two.
Once it had become law it would be a criminal offence
with very heavy penalties for anyone to transport her
across the Union's boundaries by land or air. She had to
make her decision almost immediately, either to stay in
South Africa unable to do the work she was qualified to do
or to leave her country and try to find fulfilment elsewhere.
She chose the latter. But I shall never forget the hour or
two of discussion we had together when she was struggling
to see some light, to make the right decision, knowing it
would alter the whole course of her life.

Before she left, her workers at Entokozweni organised
the protest meeting which I have described, a meeting
which she could not attend without arrest and punishment. Two or three hundred people on the dry and deso-
late veldt at Alexandra on a Sunday morning; the police in
their car, lounging and listening at the same time; a small
group of men appearing unexpectedly with the black,
green, and yellow flag of the African National Congress.
It was not a very impressive gathering by any standards.
Yet as I sat waiting my turn to speak I thought how wonderful it was really. How wonderful that here in Nationalist South Africa, in the heart of a "black spot," in a place

where African nationalism itself is at its strongest, a protest meeting should be held, a protest called and addressed by Africans (I was the only European speaker) because a white woman was being forcibly removed from amongst them after only three and a half years in their midst. Perhaps it only seems wonderful to those of us who live in the Union. And perhaps the only way of putting it into its context is to imagine the unimaginable—to think of a group of two or three hundred white South Africans protesting against the removal of an African. It is unthinkable. It could not happen. Such is the measure of European folly and wickedness that it is hard indeed to believe there is a solution.

Oliver Tambo and Helen Navid are personal friends of mine. That is why I have told their story to illustrate one aspect of the attack upon personal freedom in our country today. But they represent so many more who, in one way or another, are "buried alive." Freedom of movement no longer exists in its own right in South Africa. It is a privilege conferred or withheld by those who presently guide the destinies of the state.

And even the shock of some fresh incident seems to have lost its power to disturb the great mass of European citizens; they have grown used to the idea of a controlled and limited freedom; they have grown used to servitude.

One of the objects dearest to my heart is that of trying to open up to African boys and girls a wider and a fuller life. It seems to me that that is part of the meaning of the Christian faith itself, springing from a belief in the fact that God became man and, if He was prepared to pour His fullness into human nature, then human nature itself must be capable of such richness, must be made to receive it. Within South Africa itself it is hard indeed to open up any fields of opportunity except for a few. So it was with tremendous joy that I received a letter from the United States (again through Alan Paton) offering a bursary at Kent School, Connecticut, to any boy I chose. The offer could scarcely have been more generous or more opportune. Kent, I remembered, was one of the best schools in America: an Anglican foundation with a very strong Catholic tradition and with a very notable record of achievement in sport as well as in other directions. It had opened its doors to Negroes in the States and now wanted an African boy to share its treasures. All expenses would be paid, and he could come at once by air.

Naturally I was as careful as I knew how to be in selecting the boy. He had to be not only intelligent but adaptable, a good mixer, a lad whose home background would be not too far removed from that of the boys with whom he would soon be living. When I chose Stephen Ramasodi it was because I believed him to have all the right qualifications. I knew, of course, that there might be grave difficulties over getting him a passport. I knew, too, that if my own name were connected with him it would only intensify the difficulties. So in all the negotiations which followed, I asked the headmaster of our school to sign the letters and to do whatever else was required. Nothing, however, could disguise the fact that Stephen was at St. Peter's School, Rosettenville; and the police were well aware that of that school I was the superintendent.

The application was sent in in April. Three weeks later the boy was called for a police interrogation. A day or two after that he received a letter: "With reference to your proposed visit to the United States, we regret we are not prepared to issue a Certificate of Character." That was all.

Stephen is a lad of sixteen, not at all interested in poli-

149

tics, never in any way connected with crime, his father the principal of a government school. The Certificate of Character which would have cleared the way for a passport was refused for no reason: of that I am certain. But Stephen was at school at St. Peter's, Rosettenville. However, I was not prepared to let this refusal deter me, and after inquiring at the American Consulate whether they would give him a visa without the certificate, and having been assured that they would, I pressed forward with the application. It would be tedious to describe in detail the endless formalities, the weekly inquiries, the interventions of influential people which had to be suffered during the following two months. As I have already said, a passport, like freedom, is in South Africa a privilege conferred by the state, not a right possessed by the subject. I began to get desperate when the time of Stephen's departure for America drew near and still there was no indication that he was free to go. Each time I made inquiries I was told that a decision would be made the following week. I knew that in fact the decision would not be made at all unless it was forced upon the authorities. The only way I could hope to succeed would be by some pressure from public opinion both within and without South Africa. Fortunately I had many friends in the press and I informed them, and all foreign correspondents I could reach, of the whole situation. When the passport was refused, every newspaper in the country and many in the United States and in England had the facts and used them. For the first time, the government issued a statement giving reasons for its refusal. "It would not be in the best interests of the boy. . . ." He would return to his own country "with a shattered dream. . . . He was too young to benefit from such a bursary at present. . . ."

The fact that his parents desired him to go and were prepared if necessary for him never to return; the fact that in America Stephen would be able to choose a profession closed to him in South Africa; the fact that he was going to a church school when in the Union almost all church schools had ceased to exist because of the Bantu Education Act; the fact that for months he had set his heart on this marvellous adventure—all these things counted for nothing. The state had decided. The state knew best. The state, where Africans are concerned, always knows best. And if, in the opinion of the minister, Stephen Ramasodi must remain behind South Africa's "Iron Curtain," then there was nothing more to be said.

I took a different view of the situation. It seemed, and seems, to me such an outrageous violation of the whole Christian doctrine of man that I cannot rest until I have done all that lies in my power to overthrow the decision. Perhaps when this book appears in print I shall have succeeded; perhaps again I shall have failed. I have faith! But at least no one in South Africa will be in ignorance of the principles involved in the matter. The Archer-Shea case in England, so brilliantly re-created in *The Winslow Boy*, has been an inspiration to me in this equally vital struggle for justice. It is a struggle I truly enjoy when it centres, as it does here, upon a particular person. Somehow, then, lifted away from abstract theorising, one can see it more clearly; one can realise that to acquiesce is treason not merely to one's ideals but to one's God. And besides, I *know* Stephen, and I know the hidden treasures and ambitions, at least a little, which are in his own heart. Whilst the passport negotiations were dragging on I had to go to Southern Rhodesia for a fortnight. At the same time Stephen had to go into hospital for a minor operation. I had a letter from him, written just after the operation. The anaesthetic had somehow gone wrong; there had been a crisis, and oxygen was necessary to get him round. "They told me," he wrote, "that I nearly died. But of course I knew I should not die. God could not possibly disappoint me about America. . . ."

God could not. Dr. Verwoerd could. And did.

There is, of course, an underlying unity about the stories of Oliver, Helen, and Stephen. They are three examples of a simple development that has taken place in South Africa over the past few years. Quite apart from the fifty-seven citizens who are unable to get passports, there are scores, indeed hundreds, of citizens whose freedom of movement is so restricted as to be nonexistent in the true sense of the word "freedom." Using the Suppression of Communism Act or the Criminal Law Amendment Act or the Public Safety Act or the Native Urban Areas Act, it is possible to make a man a prisoner in his own town. It is equally possible to deport him from his own town to an isolated dorp in the back veldt. It is not only possible, it happens quite often. And those whose stories I have told are not in any way the worst examples I could quote. We shall see worse things happening in the course of the next few years, but we shall perhaps no longer count them worse because we shall have lost the taste for freedom. It is already fast slipping from us. "Eternal vigilance" is too high a price for South Africans to pay. What is astonishing about this situation is not that it exists (for a nationalism such as ours is bound to produce it) but that it exists with so little protest. It prompts me to ask two questions, and the first of them is this: "What price Commonwealth citizenship?" The Statute of Westminster, in conferring freedom upon the Dominions to develop towards full nationhood, conferred freedom upon them also to remain within or to contract out of the Commonwealth. South Africa chose the former at that time and has continued to abide by her choice. In so doing she has received many benefits, economic, strategic, and cultural; she has also made her material contribution to the wealth and to the defence of the society of nations to which she belongs. But today, with a government determined not only upon a republican form of state but upon a racial policy totally at variance with that of every other country in the Commonwealth, the question has relevance. "What price Commonwealth citizenship?" or rather, "What use?" Presumably the non-European peoples of South Africa *are* reckoned to be citizens, if not of their own country, at least of that wider society which acknowledges the Queen to be its head? But to what end? They are unable to move freely in their own land; they are unable to move out of it, even into adjacent territories acknowledging the same Sovereign. In the making of laws which restrict their freedom they have no voice and no means whatever of making their views known. In the most essential issues which affect their liberty they have no simple access to the courts; in many such issues no access and no appeal whatever.

It may seem ridiculously naïve to English or American ears to hear, as I have constantly heard, the question: "But can't the Queen help us?" Yet there is a realism behind that question which we shall ignore to our peril. There is no purpose in a loyalty either to Queen or Commonwealth if neither meets your life at any point. There is a fearful cynicism about the catch phrases "free association of free peoples," "constitutional sovereignty," and the like when you are trying to explain to an intelligent African boy why he cannot hold a British passport or move out of the country to complete his education. In fact—let us acknowledge it frankly—to the African in South Africa, Commonwealth citizenship means nothing. It seems only to accentuate an ugly truth that, somehow or other, his Sovereign must condone the state of servitude in which he lives.

The second question I would ask is even more fundamental, at least to Christians. It is with that question, essentially, that the whole of this book is concerned. Why, if the person is of infinite dignity in the sight of God, does the Church accept so complacently the constant invasions upon personal liberty which occur in South Africa?

Let me be explicit. I do not mean by "the Church" simply the hierarchy, the archbishops and bishops, the leaders of the various denominations which claim to be Christian bodies. I mean the Church in its Pauline sense as that living organism which has "many members" and which is also the Divine Society, the whole family of God.

It is but rarely in history that the hierarchy takes a prophetic view or a prophetic initiative against evil. Perhaps that is because its chief function is to guard the truth rather than to proclaim it. A Thomas à Becket, a Faulhaber, a William Temple are conspicuous because they occur so infrequently. They are in no way typical. Yet when evil appears, and especially when evil shows itself in an attack upon personal freedom, surely then, if ever, the Christian conscience should awake and should see to it that the Church not only speaks but acts! Nothing of the kind has happened in South Africa. We like to think it has. We like to think that "the voice of the Church" uttering through official channels its condemnation of the different acts or measures is a proof of its vigour and its life. Yet we know very well that these utterances have been totally ineffective

154

in preventing inroads upon personal freedom and that when particular persons have been attacked and shackled in this way no united effort has been made by the Church to aid them. The blunt truth is that the Church, the ordinary Christian man and woman, is not prepared to regard the state as an aggressor in South Africa. The Church is conniving at a policy which openly proclaims itself one of racial domination, of "white supremacy," of *baasskap*, because it fears that any effective or determined opposition will lose it the allegiance of its white members. The Church is in the deadly grip of fear; it is mesmerised by the power it thinks it sees in the hands of the government; it sits patiently, like the rabbit before the cobra, awaiting the next move and hoping (perhaps even praying) for a diversion which will allow it to scuttle to its den unharmed.

In the meanwhile personal liberty has reached vanishing point, and that human dignity which the Church is pledged to protect can hardly survive.

"Like a mighty army moves the Church of God," we sing with gusto and emotion. We do not believe a word of it. And because we do not believe a word of it, African Christians in the next two generations will find it very hard indeed to justify their allegiance.

IX. Education for Servitude

WHEN THE Ministry for Ecclesiastical Affairs was set up in Germany on July 16, 1935, it was emphasised that "Adolf Hitler's government does not fight against churches or religious denominations. It rather gathers them under its wings for protection, whenever they have mental tasks to perform. . . ."

The report of the Eiselen Commission on Native Education, appointed in 1949 and providing the basis for the Bantu Education Act, said, amongst other things: ". . . the Commission . . . expresses the opinion that the best results are obtainable in education as elsewhere from co-operation and that in accepting public grants for educational purposes the Churches become the trustees and AGENTS OF THE STATE whose business it is to educate the people. . . ." (E.R. para. 607.)

In another context the report states: "The aims of Bantu education are the development of character and intellect, and the equipping of the child for his future work and surroundings," a statement expanded and clarified by the Minister of Native Affairs, Dr. Verwoerd, when he said in the Senate: "The school must equip him [the native] to meet the demands which the economic life of South Africa WILL IMPOSE UPON HIM. . . . There is no place for the native in European society above the level of certain forms of labour."

"The racial state," wrote Adolf Hitler in his early days of ebullience, "must build up its entire educational work, in the first instance not on the pumping in of empty knowledge, but on the development of healthy bodies." One final quotation from Dr. Verwoerd, revealing because it was made in the midst of debate when introducing the bill itself: "I want to remind Honourable Members that if the native in South Africa today, in any kind of school in existence, is being taught to expect that he will live his adult life under a policy of equal rights, he is making a big mistake."

There can be no question that, of all *apartheid* legislation during the past eight years of Nationalist rule, the Bantu Education Act is by far the most important and by far the most deadly in its effect. Yet in fact that act passed through both Houses with the greatest ease and with the minimum of opposition except from one or two of the native representatives. Today it is being implemented efficiently and very swiftly all over the country. Yet its consequences will be so grave for the African people that they may take a generation or more to recover from them.

One of the reasons why the Bantu Education Act caused so little stir when it was passing through its various stages in Parliament was because so few white South Africans had any real knowledge of the state of African education anyhow. I would guarantee that nine out of ten, if asked, would have said that the native schools were run by the government. Nine out of ten would have had no conception either of the type of education given or the method of its financing or of the colour of the teachers' skins. As I have already said elsewhere, the only real interest of the European in native education lies in the master-servant relationship: in the production of a sufficient standard of literacy for efficient and obedient subjection. It is therefore necessary, if the full implications of the Bantu Education Act are to be understood, to give very briefly a picture of the situation as it was before the act came into force on April 1, 1955.

In the first place, at a conservative estimate, not more than one third of the African children of schoolgoing age were (or are) in school at all. In many districts the proportion is probably nearer one in five. There is no compulsory education for the African and of course no age limit. Of those who were able to get into school, an extremely high percentage left at very low standards. In 1948, for instance, over 50 per cent of the children were in the sub-standards: only 3.48 per cent were in standard six (the top form in the elementary school). The reason for this leakage is not far to seek, for in a society where families are large and incomes small the sooner the children can go out to work, the quicker there will be some relief economically for the whole household. No one, therefore, could look with complacency on the existing state of affairs. There was need for immediate action and reform. There was need, above all, for generous state aid financially. (It is not without significance that only £2.66 is spent annually on every African child of schoolgoing age. The corresponding figure for the European child is £43.88.) Certainly there was need for reform. And those of us who had been involved in African education as superintendents of mission schools had been urging such reform for many years without avail. We knew that the pioneering days were over; that it was fantastic to imagine that any purely voluntary organisation such as a church or a missionary society could alone handle or be responsible for the educating of a nation, still less of a nation so avid for education as the African people. Yet, in fact, the position was that in 1945 there were 4360 mission schools and only 230 government schools, and, of those 230 government schools, four fifths had been built only within the previous twenty years. The process had been what one would expect. Over a hundred years ago, when European missions started educational work in South Africa, they started it alone. They had to erect the buildings, pay the teachers, superintend the school in every detail, try to give to it the particular Christian "colour" for which it existed.

As the years passed, so their standards improved. From the open-air lesson under the gum tree they progressed to the Kimberley-brick classroom with one side open to the sun and the wind. (There are in the country plenty of such schools to this day.) But soon, as the demand increased and as it was proved that the African could "take" education in a big way, it was obvious that far more money and far better buildings would be required. The great institutions like Lovedale, Mariannhill, Adams, and the rest began to emerge not only as buildings with a dignity of their own but as schools with a character, as places where names spelt tradition. And from those schools Africans also emerged with ideals moulded in the pattern of Western Christian culture and with ambitions . . . with ambitions. . . .

Meanwhile the process of industrialisation in South Africa, as everywhere else in the modern world, had created a permanent and growing African population in the great cities. Johannesburg and the Reef at first, then Durban, Port Elizabeth, East London, all acted as magnets and drew thousands of labourers from the scorched and eroded countryside to the vital, vigorous, and often vicious towns. Schools again became an essential endeavour for all Christian bodies working in the urban areas. Thousands of pounds were invested in buildings and thousands of hours in the work of superintendence. It was not until 1925 that any considerable sums were voted by the state to aid the missions in their colossal endeavours. From that date onwards, however, every mission received grants-in-aid and corresponding state control began to be exercised. From haphazard beginnings a system was developed whereby each of the four provinces was responsible for the supervision of its African schools, for the syllabuses taught therein, and for the inspectorate. Money was voted by the state to each province for this purpose. The newer system fell under the control of the Minister of Education. But in fact practically all capital expenditure on buildings —the addition of new schools or new classrooms, the day-to-day administration of the institutions—still rested with the missions. Whereas no mission could continue to exist without state aid (teachers' salaries and school equipment being its chief purpose), 90 per cent of African education was, at every level from primary to teacher-training, in the hands of one or other of the missionary bodies—until March 31, 1955. That it was hopelessly inadequate to the present situation no one, least of all the Christian missionary, would wish to deny. At the beginning of every year we had the heartbreaking task of turning away thousands of children from our schools because there was no room for them. We had to watch the melancholy effects of a fearful overcrowding in the classrooms, particularly in the lower grades. We knew that many of our buildings were far too primitive for the needs of today, yet we simply had not the money with which to replace them. We tried to cope with the tragedy of the out-of-school child by starting afternoon schools, for which the parents paid fees, and out of these fees teachers' salaries of a sort could be met.

In the meanwhile the African people themselves were determined to meet the situation somehow; to see to it, if they possibly could, that their children received *some* education, however meagre. Empty garages, disused church halls, the back yards of private houses became private schools. By a strange irony there were quite a large number of teachers out of work, because, although only a third of the children were in school, there were no schools for the rest to go to. Teachers were there; classrooms were not. Many women, trained for the teaching profession, accepted salaries of £2.10s. or £3 a month and taught the children in their private schools. They had to be heroic in their sense of vocation: nothing else would have held them to their task. Many times I have gone round to the school in Tucker Street, an old crumbling red brick chapel, its windows broken, its wooden floor curving and cracking under the weight of children sitting there, a hundred, two hundred perhaps, their slates in their hands, no desks, no benches, no blackboards, no books. . . . Just the teacher sitting at a rickety wooden table, trying to hold their attention . . . "Say after me . . . c-a-t . . . say it. . . ." There are at this present moment, and in spite of the penalties now imposed by law on illicit private schools, thousands of African children who will owe their literacy at least to this struggling and unrewarded band of women.

Such was the situation at the end of the first century or so of missionary struggle in the field of African education. It presented an exceedingly grim problem, but it had its encouraging features. It was quite clear that, given the opportunity, the African school could produce the goods: not in great numbers, obviously, for there were always enormous obstacles, economic and otherwise, to overcome.

But a steady stream of cultured (as opposed to merely "educated") Africans was leaving the schools, proceeding to Fort Hare or the Witwatersrand or Cape Town universities, and beginning to make its mark on society. We at St. Peter's, Rosettenville, had been the first school in the Transvaal at which Africans could take Matric. That was in the early 1930's. Already we had produced priests, doctors, lawyers, and teachers of high quality by any standards. One of our old boys is presently lecturer in applied mathematics at Fort Hare and was described by his tutor as one of the most brilliant mathematicians he had ever taught. But every mission institution of any size could boast a similar record. Our problem lay not so much in turning out the men and women who could make progress in the professions: it lay in finding the opportunity (and that meant the money *and* the opening) for such fulfilment. The worst days in the year for me were always those at the end of the exams, when the children whom I had known and loved at school came to ask me what they were to do next . . . what they could do to further their studies . . . what profession they could make their own. But that is another story, and in a sense this book is a comment upon it also.

I have tried to show as fairly as I can the background of the Bantu Education Act. And surely, on any at all objective analysis of that background, three things emerge quite clearly:

First, the fact that, apart from missionary effort, there would have been no African education in South Africa at all.

Second, the fact that by 1930–40 the pioneering work of the missions had been done and the position reached where state schools and far more generous state subsidisation were both essential if progress were to be maintained.

Third, the fact that in equity the missions had the right to guard what they had so laboriously won for the African people: an educational system which, however imperfect, was based upon the Christian faith itself and the traditions of Western Christian culture and civilisation.

In 1949 the government appointed a Commission on Native Education, and its chairman was Dr. W. W. M. Eiselen, a former Chief Inspector of Native Education in the Transvaal. No single missionary and no one representing the mission schools was a member of the commission. Neither, of course, was there any representative of the African people. The commission spent some two years hearing evidence, and when its report was issued it was a massive volume of over two hundred foolscap pages printed in double columns. No one could criticise the thoroughness or the factual accuracy of the report. It gave a complete and most exhaustive statement of the history of African education.

As soon as there had been time for digestion, the South African Institute of Race Relations sponsored a conference at the university to consider the findings. I was present at the conference, which was notable for the eminence of its speakers and chairman, notable also for the apparent unwillingness of the government to send anything like a representative group, notable also for the unanimous rejection of the basic principles underlying the report.

"In general," ran the summary of Aims of Bantu Education, "the function of education is to transmit the culture of a society from its more mature to its immature members, and in so doing develop their powers" (para. 754); and again: "Education must be co-ordinated into a definite and carefully planned policy for the development of Bantu societies"; and again: "The Bantu child comes to school with a basic physical and psychological endowment which differs . . . *so slightly if at all* [italics mine] from that of the European child that no special provision has to be made in educational theory or basic aims." It was not difficult for the skilled and highly experienced educationists taking part in the conference to point out the strange contradictions of a report which on the one hand emphasised so strongly the need to preserve "traditional Bantu culture" and on the other could not produce any concrete evidence that that culture existed or was worth preserving. It was not hard, either, to criticise that amazing paradox which with one voice proclaimed that the African child had no real physical or psychological differences from the European and with another shouted more aggressively that the type of education given to the one was totally unsuitable to the other.

The Eiselen report was condemned, however, not so much for the detailed proposals for reform which it advocated, many of which are of obvious merit and indeed of necessity. The Institute of Race Relations—a body which is very widely representative of "liberal" opinion in South Africa and which could not be called specifically Christian in its approach—condemned the report for its basic assumptions. It was these that were wrong and that, if acted upon, could give a wrong bias to education for generations. What, then, are these assumptions? What is their inherent evil? They can really be reduced to one quite simple statement; a statement which, I feel sure, neither

Dr. Eiselen nor Dr. Verwoerd will quarrel with. In sum, the Eiselen report recommended and the Bantu Education Act implemented the creation of a new form of education in South Africa. It was to be called "Bantu Education." It was to be separate entirely from education itself. To make that separation it was to be geared into a whole new plan for Bantu development, of which it would be but one element; important, but secondary, to the whole scheme.

To make quite certain that "Bantu Education" would be of a new and other parentage than education, the minister responsible for it would be not the Minister of Education but, of course, the Minister of Native Affairs. In other words, the Bantu Education Act and the Eiselen commission report on which it is based are the essential and absolutely logical corollaries of the *apartheid* policy of South Africa. It is essential to that policy, because unless you can begin by indoctrinating the children you will have little hope of persuading the adult. If, as I believe, *apartheid* is itself subordinate to the idea of "white supremacy now and always," it is certainly most necessary to start with the young: the younger the better. It is logical, too, to use the educational machinery provided for you in a way most certain to discredit those who have provided it; by assuring the African that the missionary was making such a mess of things that it needed a benevolent government to clear it up; to give you what the churches were not able or were not willing to give—an education suited to the Bantu environment, conditioned by the Bantu tradition, based as far as possible upon Bantu tribal ethics. Such an education must necessarily, as Dr. Verwoerd said in the Senate in June 1954, "stand with both feet in the Reserve." It must also be freed, once for all, from the malign influence of Christian missions.

The Bantu Education Act is a short document. It states little beyond the fact that from the date of its enactment the control of African education passes to the Department of Native Affairs.

In August 1954 all mission superintendents received the first of a number of official circulars stating how that transfer would take place. It amounted to an ultimatum, for the choice given to the missions was a simple one. By December 1954 the mission schools and institutions must either hand themselves over entirely to the state and lose their identity as mission schools, or they must accept a cut in subsidy which would allow them temporarily to continue in existence but which would in a short while be so extended as to reduce the subsidy to nothing. No teacher-training institutions could continue under the control of missions. No private schools could exist without the permission of the minister. Heavy penalties would be imposed on any individual or group attempting to evade the regulations. This circular was, in effect, the death of African mission schools. We at St. Peter's had already discussed our plans in the light of the Eiselen report. We knew what we should do, and within a week of receiving our circular we had notified the government of our intention to close the school. We were fully aware of what we were doing and of the hardship and suffering it would involve for many of our children and teachers. Yet we believed that only by demonstrating in a clear and unmistakable fashion our opposition to the whole basis of the act could we best continue to serve the African people. We could neither accept the principle of *apartheid* education nor assist in its implementation in any way.

I wrote an article for the *Star* and subsequently a pamphlet called *The Death of a School*, in which I tried to explain the position to the public; a public almost totally unaware of the issues involved and, where aware of them, almost totally apathetic.

In the meanwhile the various Christian bodies were meeting and expressing their views on the subject. Five months was not long for making up one's mind on how to meet this new and crushing development. It was not unlike the position of the patient awaiting the amputation of both legs and being told at the same time that he must look for a new job. Every church authority in the country, with the single exception of the Dutch Reformed Church (who, to do it justice, had consistently urged state control for all mission schools), condemned the act and the measures which flowed from the act. The minister was approached directly and indirectly by the different churches and urged to reconsider his decisions. The tragic mistake, as I shall always believe, lay in the failure of the churches to act together. I am convinced that had, say, the Methodists, the Roman Catholics, the Presbyterians, and the Anglicans united for once on this single issue, had they approached the Prime Minister and stated that in conscience they could not co-operate in the implementation of the act, at least some major concessions would have been won.

Whilst each church individually protested, argued against, and condemned the rape of its schools, none, apparently, could take the initiative in urging a total refusal to surrender. A few institutions followed the same line as St. Peter's. The rest pursued a policy of "wait and see." Already, from within the mission camp, voices were heard whispering the insidious and fatal fallacies which so many ears were longing to hear. "After all, it may not work out so badly. . . . The inspectors are good men. . . . Verwoerd does not have anything to do with the working out of the plan. . . . African teachers won't *teach* inferiority. . . . Anyhow, what can we do?" It was the voice of Vichy. It is that voice which, by and large, has prevailed.

Although the Anglican Church had condemned the act as heartily as every other Christian body, when it came to the point of deciding how to translate her opposition into reality it was another story.

Of course we were placed in a cruel dilemma: a dilemma all the more cruel because it involved making decisions which would affect the lives of children, of those who could have no possible part in the decisions or in their effect. If we refused to hand over our school buildings to the government, thousands of children would be on the street. If we accepted the temporary subsidy, we could neither afford to keep the majority of our schools open, nor could we envisage any hope of continuance when the subsidy was withdrawn (in 1957, as we now know). Moreover, we would simply be aiding the government by making it easier for them to take control, giving them time to prepare their administrative machinery. In the end, every diocese of the Anglican Church in South Africa save one—Johannesburg—capitulated to the demands of the government. It was better, said the Archbishop of Cape Town, for children to have a rotten education than none at all.

With the exception of the Roman Catholic and Seventh-Day Adventist churches, every other missionary body took the same line. It would be most presumptuous and most impertinent to pass judgment on any of them for so doing. I am personally convinced, however, and every day that passes deepens my conviction, that the Bishop of Johannesburg was right. History, I believe, will endorse my opinion and will vindicate his courageous and lonely stand on principle.

The Johannesburg Diocese, St. Peter's School, and one or two other institutions (notably Modderpoort in the Free State and Adam's in Natal) have chosen the path of "death with honour." For doing so we have been soundly rated not only by State Information officers (that was only to be expected) but by many of our fellow Christians and by most of those who, a few months ago, were loudest in their condemnation of the Bantu Education Act. The hardest thing, perhaps, in the world is to stand by the principle to the end and, "having done all, to stand." It is made much harder when one is caught up into the deep and bitter suffering of the people one loves most dearly.

The suffering of the African people through the Bantu Education Act is peculiarly hard both to assess and to describe. Perhaps I am in as good a position as any European to try to do so; and it is most important that someone should try, for it is freely claimed by the government that Bantu Education is not only most acceptable to the African people but that they themselves have said so. It is possible to point to the fact that the transference of schools has taken place with little trouble; that the boycott organised by the African National Congress has failed, except in one or two centres; that the parents have themselves refused to take part in the boycott; that the school boards, composed of Africans, are beginning to get down to work; that in public speeches various teachers of standing have acclaimed the Bantu Education Act and have rejoiced at the end of missionary control. The Information Office of the Department of Native Affairs has devoted a great deal

of time and energy to the whole issue, and both in South
Africa and overseas the propaganda line is that the African people, if left to themselves and the government,
would be more than content with the Bantu Education
Act. It is only agitation, "liberalists" (a new and now familiar term of abuse), and "misguided clerics" who create
opposition and mistrust. What is the truth?

As I have already tried to make clear, no one dare claim
that mission schools were perfect, were even within meas-
urable distance of perfection. There were certainly excellent reasons for reform. But, most of all, there were
excellent reasons for a more generous financial policy
which would have enabled the missions to equip themselves for their colossal task more adequately. There was,
too, a time, which I remember well, when teachers were
dissatisfied not only with their salaries but also with their
conditions of service in mission schools. They had many
reasons for such dissatisfaction. But there was never a time
when it was possible to compare government schools, and
conditions in those schools, with mission schools, for by
and large, government schools did not exist.

It is, therefore, of some significance that today, in
Sophiatown, where there are many schools now operating
under the Bantu Education authority, there is an opportunity to make comparison. Our Anglican school closed in
obedience to the bishop's decision to refuse co-operation
with government. It re-opened a month later as a private
school without subsidy and therefore had to charge a fee
of ten shillings per month in order to pay its teachers. In
spite of the fact that education in all the other schools is
free, this school has an attendance of six hundred children
and a waiting list as long again.

The truth is that the parents have no choice; or, rather,

they are faced with the same hideous dilemma: "Bantu education" or the street. The African National Congress, foreseeing the immense difficulties and the problem confronting the people, decided nevertheless to urge a total boycott of all schools. It was to be left to each area to decide on the most suitable moment for this action. In certain places, Alexandra Township, Brakpan, Western Native Township, Germiston, Benoni (all the Reef), the boycott was considerable. Thousands of children stayed away from school on a particular day in protest. It is, after all, a technique not unknown in other countries, and it is in South Africa absolutely within the law, for there is no compulsory education. Nevertheless, Dr. Verwoerd decided to regard the boycott as an act of rebellion. The seven thousand children who took part in it were told that they would not be allowed in any school again. The parents of all African children were warned that any further attempts at such a demonstration would lead to permanent exclusion from school for any children allowed to take part in it. Schools affected by the boycott lost their teachers' salary grants, and the teachers lost their jobs.

In face of such drastic measures, it was small cause for wonder that the boycott as a whole failed to materialise. To plead that children are always politically innocent is of no avail with the government of South Africa. Boycott becomes a crime because it means opposition to government policy. The African child is penalised in the way that hurts most, by deprivation of schooling, because he is involved in a protest against *apartheid*.

In certain areas the boycott was effective. For several days schools were empty. Some seven thousand children were kept out of the classrooms, and their teachers were idle. Those children (or rather their parents) were told that they must not attend school again. Teachers were warned by the government not to accept "boycott" children in their institutions. The door of education must be closed in punishment for the crime of rebellion—of rebellion not against law, but against Dr. Verwoerd.

Not long after all this had happened I went to see for myself what was being done for these children—innocents who had now been driven permanently on to the streets of their locations to join the already vast mass of out-of-school Africans. I went first to Benoni, one of the older African locations on the Reef. I drove into the heart of the township and stopped the car outside a dilapidated building which had once been a cinema. With Robert Resha, a Congress leader in the Western Areas, I entered the building. It was very dark. What light there was filtered through two holes high up in the walls, where bricks had been removed just for that purpose. At first it was impossible to see; my eyes had to grow accustomed to the gloom. Then gradually the light fell upon a mass of heads, upon a crowd of children of all sizes, of all ages, gathered round a table. Seated at the table was a young African woman, trying to demonstrate some game, trying to keep fifty, a hundred children interested, or at least quiet. There were two or three other groups playing round the hall, or sitting on the dusty floor arranging letters into an alphabet, or just sitting. . . . There was no blackboard; there were no school books; there were no benches. . . . This was a "Cultural Club," and such things as would equip a school would immediately make it illegal.

At Brakpan, a few miles farther on, the Cultural Club was meeting in the open air. As we drove up to the square there was a shout and a rush of children—the enrolment that morning was over five hundred—all with their thumbs raised in the Congress salute. Five or six ex-teachers had organised them into groups. They were playing games, making dolls out of pipe cleaners, knitting, sewing, even mending shoes. Here, as at Benoni, there was hardly any equipment for club work, nothing that could suggest a school. Yet there was an *élan*, a vitality about the whole place which was infectious. "When our children pass the children from the Bantu Education School," said one of the organisers, "they put their thumbs up and cry out, 'Verwoerd, Verwoerd . . .'" Before we left Brakpan, the children were brought together into a semi-circle to sing to us. This, of course, is a familiar enough ending to every "official" visit to a school in Africa. So were the tunes we heard. Only the words were different. "There are only two ways for Africa," they sang, "one way leads to Congress, and one way to Verwoerd. . . ." We drove away still hearing the chorus of their last song, sung with great gusto and obvious enjoyment: "Down with Bantu Education. Down with Bantu Education. . . ." Some of the singers were only seven years old.

At present it is a very small minority, both of teachers and parents (and consequently of children), who openly oppose the Bantu Education Act or at least who are prepared to risk penalties for doing so.

The government claims to have won the support of the great majority of Africans for the new system. It bases its claim on the fact that the new school boards are beginning to function, on the fact that parents as a whole have refused to take part in boycotts, and on the continued acceptance by most of the teachers of their new status.

I am convinced, however, that the Bantu Education Act and its implementation are the beginning of a resistance movement amongst the African people; that, however outwardly compliant they may be, there burns beneath the surface a fire of fierce resentment which one day will get out of control. It cannot be otherwise. Bantu Education is one of the chief instruments of a policy of racialism whose avowed aim is the establishment of an enduring white supremacy. It is, indeed, an education for servitude. But it has come too late. It has come when, after more than a century of Christian education, the door is already open to a wider and freer world of vision. It will take more than Dr. Verwoerd to close that door.

X. Out, Damned Spot

It is the morning of February 10, 1955. I stand once again where I have stood so many times before, at the low altar step in St. Mary Magdalene's chapel in the Church of Christ the King, Sophiatown. We begin the Preparation: "I will go unto the altar of God . . . even into the God of my joy and gladness. . . . Our help standeth in the name of the Lord . . . Who hath made heaven and earth. . . ." I notice it is Michael who kneels beside me to make the responses . . . how many times has he knelt just there in the past years? . . . And behind me, I know without looking, there will be Seth Pilane, who never misses his daily Mass; there will be perhaps ten or fifteen members of the Guild; there will be the Sisters and some of the servers. . . . It is still dark outside, for it is only five o'clock and another hour to sunrise. Normally I would know exactly the appearance of the street outside, the familiar sounds of dawn in Sophiatown: the first steps of men walking down the hill to the bus stop, the clop-clop of the horses as they draw old Makudu's cart out of his yard for another day's coal-hawking, a baby crying, a cock crowing, distant voices as people greet each other in the half light.

But today is not normal: not at all. In fact, I am saying Mass an hour early because it is "the Day"; because it is the beginning of the end of Sophiatown; because from now nothing will ever be the same again in this little corner of

South Africa; because today the great Removal is beginning, and all the people I know and the houses they live in will soon be scattered, and Sophiatown itself will crumble into dust.

"The Word was made flesh and dwelt among us, and we beheld His glory, the glory of the only begotten by the Father, full of grace and truth." I walk back to the sacristy and unvest, say my thanksgiving for this blessed and most strengthening Food, then out into the street. By the gate there is already a little group of men, waiting. They are the African correspondents of many of the British and overseas newspapers. There seem to be dozens of cameras, though it is still so dark that a photograph would be hard to get. A light rain is falling. Suddenly, from the corner out of sight, where Edward Road meets Ray Street down the dip, there comes a sound I have never heard in Sophiatown before. It is the noise of men marching. The staccato "Hep, Hi, Hep . . . Hep, Hi, Hep . . ." getting louder; and in a moment they breast the hill and draw level with us. A flash bulb goes off. A detachment of African police under European command marches raggedly but purposefully past us down the hill. People appear from their houses in the darkness and stand, chattering but subdued, to watch this new and unfamiliar sight.

I walked with Douglas Brown of the *Daily Telegraph* and Leonard Ingalls of the New York *Times* down Victoria Road to see what was happening. It was beginning to get light, but the rain was coming down hard. The bus queues were already forming, and as we passed, many of the men gave the Congress sign and greeted me cheerfully. One or two others ran across the road and shook me by the hand. It all looked very normal. It was only when we got to Toby Street that we began to understand how things were shaping: that we knew for certain that the REMOVAL, so long talked about, so often and so fiercely debated, had actually begun. On the broad belt of grass between the European suburb of Westdene and Sophiatown (we called that strip "the Colour Bar") a whole fleet of Army lorries was drawn up: a grim sight against the grey, watery sky. Lining the whole street were thousands of police, both white and black, the former armed with rifles and revolvers, the latter with the usual *assegai*. A few Sten guns were in position at various points. A V.I.P. car, containing the Commissioner of Police and a mobile wireless unit (which we afterwards discovered was in hourly contact with the minister in Cape Town) patrolled up and down.

"Where are they beginning?"

"In the yard opposite the bus station, at the bottom of Toby Street. . . . Let's go."

It was a fantastic sight. It looked more like a film set for an "atmospheric" Italian film than anything real. In the yard, military lorries were drawn up. Already they were piled high with the pathetic possessions which had come from the row of rooms in the background. A rusty kitchen stove; a few blackened pots and pans; a wicker chair; mattresses belching out their coir stuffing; bundles of heaven-knows-what; and people, soaked, all soaked to the skin by the drenching rain. Above this strange and depressing crowd, perched on top of the van of a police truck were more cameras filming the scene below. I deliberately put my arm round Robert Resha's shoulders and looked up at the camera.

"Move away there. . . . You've no right here. . . . Get out, I'm telling you. . . . Clear out of this yard." One officer was in a furious temper. Perhaps it was the rain, but I think it was the sight of me with my arm on an African shoulder. This man made a rush at one of the cameramen who was trying to get a shot of him, pushed his camera away, and might easily have broken it.

We walked up the street. Whenever I stopped, a little group of Africans gathered round me. They were *our* people. But as soon as I started chatting, a policeman would come up and order me to move on. The Minister of Justice had imposed a ban on all gatherings. A chat in the street with a few friends was a gathering. I moved on, and the process was repeated a hundred yards farther on. . . .

The first lorries began to move off for Meadowlands eight miles away to the west. The rain poured down. The Removal was definitely under way. Two thousand police, armed; many foreign correspondents; dozens of photographers; a total ban on all gatherings, including (as was thought at the time) attendance at a church service. All this to effect a slum-clearance scheme which would be of lasting benefit to the "natives"; all this to carry through a plan which anyone could see to be a good plan; all this excitement and fuss and publicity over a project which, to any sensible European in South Africa, was a crying necessity if white civilisation was to be preserved. What was it all about? What were the principles involved? What was the Western Areas Removal Scheme anyway? These questions must be answered here in view of the immense interest shown in this matter by the world at large. Nothing since Michael Scott's revelations about farming conditions at Bethal has made so great an impact on the international press. Yet today, when the removal of sixty thousand people to Meadowlands is proceeding rapidly and Sophiatown begins to look like a blitzed area in London, the moral and ethical implications of this scheme are barely understood, and if once they were debated they are now forgotten. Yet I believe that the Western Areas Removal Scheme—to give it its official name—will one day be recognised as a major issue of race relations in South Africa. We would do well to learn the lessons it has to teach.

In the first place, the Removal Scheme is no new idea. It was not even the invention of the Nationalist government. It emerged as soon as the white suburbs of Johannesburg began to spread westward and to make their first contact with old Tobiansky's "mixed" estate. It is now fifty years since Sophiatown was first occupied by Africans. It is over forty since Newclare (which is part of the Western Areas) was established and whites were specifically restricted from residing in the township. It is nearly forty years since the Johannesburg Town Council was so convinced of the non-European nature of that part of the city that it built its own location, the Western Native Township, in the heart of the area and ringed it with an iron fence. By 1920 no one would have questioned the fact that Sophiatown, Martindale, and Newclare were and always would be black. And by 1920 the industrial expansion of Johannesburg had also begun, and the Africans drawn into the city as its labour force needed homes. They found them, as they must, in Sophiatown and its neighbourhood. What was more important to many of them, they found an opportunity—rare indeed in urban Africa—for investment in real estate. Instead of living in a municipally owned location, they could live on their own plot in their own homes. And their children and their children's children could live there too. Freehold rights, even if amenities were lacking, were worth having. That was undoubtedly one of the great attractions of Sophiatown. The other was its nearness to the city. Instead of spending time and money on

181

transport, as those who lived way out at Pimville Location had to do, they were within cycling distance of their work. Altogether it was a good place to be, combining the freedom of the country with the convenience of the town. And it was healthy, too, for it stood high on a ridge of rock and you could look away towards Pretoria over open, rolling country where fresh breezes blew.

The only problem as the years passed was that of overcrowding. Industry continued to respond, particularly when South Africa went off gold. Labour was needed for the factories and the business houses of the city in a big way. And it had to be black labour, for that alone was both cheap and plentiful. Unfortunately it did not occur to Johannesburg citizens that the labour force also had to live somewhere, had to have houses. One of the effects of the race situation in South Africa has always been that blindness. Labour is labour; it is not human if it is black. It must be there, standing ready in your factory or your kitchen or your office, but it must make no demands for the necessities of life: a rooftree or an income large enough to support the home. It must have strong muscles for the job, but how they are to become strong is its own concern. It must have clean clothes and a tidy appearance in your home, but it doesn't matter where or how it is to get the water for washing or the space for drying. So Johannesburg built its factories, its flats, and its fun-fairs; it forgot to build houses for its African citizens. And Sophiatown, with its eighteen hundred "stands," began to crack at the seams with its growing population. There was some relief when another municipal location at Orlando was started. But that was needed far more rapidly than it was built. The density of population in Sophiatown continued to increase every year, even though new families moved into

Orlando as soon as the houses were finished; even though there was soon a waiting list of thousands registered with the civic authorities for vacant homes.

The expansion of Johannesburg was not restricted to its non-European labour force. The white population, too, increased, drawing men from the country by the same economic forces which have operated in every part of the world since the Industrial Revolution. And it chose to spread westward. New suburbs sprang up beyond Ferreirastown. Brixton, Newlands, Westdene: an encirclement of the non-European area had begun. White artisans occupied these suburbs for the most part, and in Westdene they were predominantly Afrikaners. By a strange irony, the group most strongly anti-African (because it has most to fear from African competition) occupied houses only a few yards from the last street in Sophiatown and looked across a strip of grass at the homes which had been established there.

By 1937 the first sounds of battle were heard, and by 1939 a city councillor whose constituency abutted on Sophiatown demanded the total removal of all non-European settlements in the Western Areas. But in view of the total failure of the City Council to build houses fast enough anywhere in Johannesburg to meet the needs of the African labour force, and also in view of the demands made on the country by the war, nothing was done. In 1944, a year after my arrival in Sophiatown, the Council approved in principle the removal of all Africans and coloureds from the area. But no attempt was made in the following years to implement the scheme, and no attempt was made either to proceed with slum clearance or to build sufficient houses for those who desperately needed them. It was during the period 1944–49 that the shanty towns emerged, and it was during that period also that the number of African families without any proper home reached catastrophic proportions. The idea of uprooting sixty thousand people who at least had a roof over their heads became ludicrous in view of the vast mass of the homeless who had to make do with shacks and shanties all round the western perimeter of the city.

The "problem" of the Western Areas was added to all the other "problems" of South Africa. But basically the issue was dead simple. It was just this: that white Johannesburg had encroached upon black Johannesburg, and so, naturally, black Johannesburg must move on. MUST MOVE ON. That is why the Western Areas Scheme is so terribly important to the Christian; or, rather, why it ought to be. An African freehold township, established for fifty years, can be uprooted and totally destroyed because it is contiguous with a European suburb. The question of right or wrong does not have any relevance. The story of Naboth's vineyard rings no bell. Arguments soundly based on economics or town planning or on history have no meaning whatsoever. If a black township stands where a white suburb wants to stand, the township must go. We can think up a justification for it afterwards.

When the Malan government was returned to power in 1948 it wasted no time in elevating the Western Areas Scheme to the level of national importance. Minister Mentz, M.P., speaking in the House of Assembly, stated solemnly that "there is not a single strand of barbed wire between my constituency (Westdene) and Sophiatown." Obviously such an appalling danger to European security could not be allowed to continue any longer. The City Council was ordered to get a move on and to implement its recommendations of 1944.

It should not be forgotten that, during the long years when the Removal Scheme was under discussion by the authorities, it was never once discussed with the people who were going to be removed; with the ratepayers of Sophiatown who, though they paid their rates, had no other contact with the municipal authorities to whom they paid them than the privilege of paying. For nearly twenty years the threat had hung over the Western Areas. Those who had invested their savings in homes for themselves and their children might lose everything; those who wanted some security, some assurance of a future, dared not risk basing it on such shifting foundations. Always, in those years, we were living in a place which was besieged by the forces of fear and uncertainty. It was this, added to the overcrowding, which imposed slum conditions on an area which, in every possible respect, was most suited to be and to remain an African suburb. It is not much of an encouragement to improve your property if, any morning, you open your newspaper and see headlines, "Western Areas Plan Approved: Black Spots to be Removed." I am convinced from my experience in Sophiatown that a great deal of the crime and of the juvenile delinquency was directly due to this sense of insecurity. If you're going to lose what you've got anyhow, why worry too much about other people's rights and property? But that is another story.

Our chief difficulty in fighting the Removal was twofold. In the first place, we had to demand and to go on demanding a genuine slum-clearance scheme. That is to say, the building of houses in a sufficient number at Orlando or elsewhere to make it possible for the sub-tenants of Sophiatown to move out and thus reduce the density of population to reasonable proportions. On the other hand, we had to keep the citizens of Johannesburg awake to the plain truth that the government's scheme was not slum clearance but robbery: robbery carried out in the interests of and under pressure from the neighbouring white suburbs: a political manoeuvre. The South African Institute of Race Relations called a conference in August 1953, to which fifty-one organisations sent representatives. The government and the City Council were also invited to attend. Both refused. "Such a conference," said the Secretary of State for Native Affairs, "should not take place . . . it will not in my opinion serve any useful purpose." Obviously, as in every other issue affecting the African people, the government had no intention of consultation and no desire to hear their point of view. THEY MUST MOVE. They are natives, so the government always knows what is best for them and does it.

Soon after this, a group of us, including Helen Navid, formed the Western Areas Protest Committee, of which I was the chairman, and went into the fight for the conscience of Johannesburg. It was our aim to work in the closest conjunction with the African National Congress and the Transvaal Indian Congress. They were to organise the people in the areas themselves; we were to reach the European suburbs and try to educate the white citizens on the true implications of the scheme. Our hope was that in this way we might at least succeed in forcing the City Council to refuse to co-operate with the government. In the meanwhile the Bishop of Johannesburg and the Citizens' Housing League were attacking the Council fiercely and persistently over its failure to build houses. It was not too difficult to point to the "shelters" at Orlando and to the Moroka Emergency Camp and to show that at least ninety thousand people were living under slum conditions quite obviously worse than anything in Sophiatown; and these slums were municipally owned. What *was* difficult was to make Johannesburg realise that there were moral issues involved; for 90 per cent of its people had never seen the places we were talking about and could not care less what happened to them.

We campaigned in the suburbs with varying success. But at least we made some progress: we made the city aware of the possible dangers involved in a compulsory removal scheme. After a great deal of shilly-shally the Council announced that it would not co-operate with the government.

Dr. Verwoerd reacted promptly and characteristically by creating a new local authority with plenary powers which would be directly responsible to him for carrying through his plans. The "black spot" of Sophiatown became for the Native Affairs Department its chief priority. Every possible use was made of propaganda to prove that those who opposed the Removal were in fact opposing slum clearance; and Meadowlands—the area chosen for the new location—became a symbol of all the paternal charity and foresight which Dr. Verwoerd so loves to proclaim as the fruit of an *apartheid* policy. This was exactly what the conscience of Johannesburg was waiting for: to be able to relax again in the comforting thought that, after all, Sophiatown was a filthy slum; Meadowlands would be a tidy and controlled location. The natives would be better off, even if they had lost freehold rights, even if they had to travel farther to their work, even if they were now in a place where government regulations and restrictions could be most vigorously imposed. It became increasingly difficult for us to get a favourable press. And naturally in consequence it became difficult to maintain European opposition. In Sophiatown itself, Congress carried on a campaign

187

of public meetings (always attended by the political branch of the C.I.D.) and of house-to-house visits. But they, too, were running into great practical difficulties. It was all very well to explain to people the meaning of the Removal and the loss of rights it must entail. It was more difficult to work out any constructive plan of opposition; for, if people resisted removal to Meadowlands, at least some alternative accommodation must be provided. And in the Western Areas there had been no accommodation for years.

Such was the position when in February the government acted. It acted with great efficiency, with overwhelming force, and with a surprise move two days earlier than was expected. Perhaps we had done our job more effectively than we knew, for the press of the world was there on that February morning; and if South Africa and Johannesburg were largely unconcerned, Sophiatown became for a time world news.

I think many people expected violent resistance to the Removal and were surprised when the lorries moved off to Meadowlands so safely and with such apparently happy travellers. I was attacked in the House of Assembly by both the Minister of Native Affairs and the Minister of Justice for having attempted to invite gangsterism and to encourage the use of armed force. Although I challenged the two ministers to repeat their statements outside the privileged forum of Parliament, neither did so. Nor did any of my ecclesiastical superiors (the Bishop of Johannesburg was away in England at the time) attempt to come to my defence. Indeed I cannot honestly say that, in the whole struggle for the upholding of principle and the resistance to oppression which the Removal meant to us, there was any very noticeably Christian opposition to the scheme.

And as soon as the move to Meadowlands had begun, the press and the people of Johannesburg made every effort to justify what they had both previously condemned. The seduction of power had worked effectively once more.

As I write these words, some thousands have left Sophia-town (the government claims ten thousand) and have settled in the new location. Many of the streets are becoming heaps of rubble. The squalid shelters, the sordid rooms have been pulled down, and the places where they stood lie open to the sun and to the sky. Beside them also lie the remains of houses which I have also known, where families lived happily and in pride of ownership. The good and the bad are destroyed together; their occupants live in the neat monotony of Meadowlands.

I do not weep for the destruction of the material which was Sophiatown. At least two thirds of it would have had to be destroyed in any scheme for the renewing of that area which we always dreamed might come to pass. I do not weep, either, simply because what I have known and greatly loved is no more. Living through two world wars at least teaches one a measure of detachment and is a reminder to all men that "here we have no abiding city." Nor do I condemn Meadowlands as a place to live. It has a pretty name. It is a pleasant site. And if you are used to locations, I suppose it bears comparison with any other. At least it is just as dull. But I weep because the Western Areas Removal Scheme and the uprooting of sixty thousand people are being carried out with the connivance of the Christian conscience of Johannesburg. I weep because in spite of all we have tried to do we have failed so utterly to uphold principle against prejudice, the rights of persons against the claims of power.

"But after all, padre," said a B.B.C. correspondent sent

to make a recording for his programme, "you must admit that Sophiatown was a slum. It was a jolly good thing it was cleared away. And I've seen Meadowlands: it's fine. They're quite happy. What are freehold rights anyway? Surely the principle isn't as important as all that? And most of the property in Sophiatown was mortgaged too. Don't you think all the fuss was a bit of a mistake? Was it fair? Is the government always wrong?" I should have liked to answer those questions over the air. But apparently that was not considered desirable. Now, when the Removal is to most people a thing of the past, it is a little late to make comments. Yet, late or not, I must try for the sake of the future and for the sake of truth itself.

Sophiatown *was* a slum. Those of us who have lived there would never wish to deny that. We have seen with our own eyes the heroism of so many of our own Christian people in their battle to fight and to overcome their environment. It would be treason to them to deny that Sophiatown was a slum. But slum conditions can be removed without the expropriation of a whole area. Indeed the greatest experts in town planning would agree that only in the last resort should you uproot people from the place they know as home; for in such uprooting you destroy not only the fabric of their houses, you destroy a living organism—the community itself. Sophiatown, then, could have been replanned and rebuilt on the same site: a model African suburb. It could have been, but for the pressure of three things. First, the pressure of white opinion and the political force it represented; second, the existence of freehold tenure and the threat of permanence which it implied; third, that which underlies every event of any racial significance in South Africa: the assumption that white "civilisation" is threatened by the very existence of an

African community in any way similar to itself. The African in the *kraal* is in his right place; so is the African in the kitchen. But the African in a "European" suburb, in a "European" house which he himself owns and is proud of: he is a menace; he must be removed.

They are happy in Meadowlands. I do not doubt it. For even in a location you can have your family and your friends about you, and that is a home of sorts, even if it is not your own. And maybe it is a far better home than the single room or the corrugated-iron shack that you have left. But beneath your happiness you know, or perhaps you only feel without knowing, a deeper uncertainty and a more profound unrest.

You have been moved to Meadowlands today. Where will you be moved to tomorrow? When white Johannesburg once more creeps up to your doorstep and you in turn become a threat to its peace and to its security, what will happen? Where does the process stop? It never stops in South Africa. There is no rest, no permanence, no future you can be sure of, for domination is an insatiable hunger. It is never satisfied, for it is never certain of itself. It can never rest, for it never knows its own final end or purpose. They are happy in Meadowlands. All right, all right, let us admit it. But one day Sophiatown will be a white suburb, or perhaps a white industrial zone, with factories and workshops standing where the rubble now lies. Its life as an African township will be forgotten. Perhaps only the names of Tobiansky's children at the street corners will remind men of its past. But it will be stolen property. And nothing that man can do will alter that. Nor, I believe, will the African people ever forget it, however happy they may be in Meadowlands, however long the years since that February morning when an army came to Sophiatown and destroyed it for ever.

XI. Comfort, Use and Protection

Man seeketh in society comfort, use and protection.
FRANCIS BACON

I HAVE tried in this book to confine myself to examples of the working out of a race-domination policy which I have actually seen or experienced. I have not drawn on press reports of incidents which might illustrate my theme perhaps more clearly. But in this chapter I shall use one such illustration because it happens to be recent and exceedingly apposite.

Nothing, I think, is more psychologically revealing than the attempt made by the government of South Africa to explain to the rest of the world the justice, the right-mindedness, and the deep understanding which guide its racial policies.

"These men," said a very well-known television commentator from America to me, "are always on the defensive. We didn't come here to have a crack at Strijdom or Verwoerd; we came to take an objective picture. But all we get is the usual stuff about whites being swamped by blacks. . . . If their policy's so good, let's hear about their policy: it ought to justify itself."

What South Africans really resent in the comments of
men like Canon Collins is the exposure of the truth; the
denuding of their carefully clothed and vested export
model of *apartheid;* the strip tease which does in fact lay
bare a great deal of unattractive, not to say indecent, motive—what they *say* they resent is the impertinence of a
foreigner passing moral judgments in ignorance of the
facts. (They cannot say that about me, for I happen to be a
South African citizen; I happen also to have lived in an
African urban area for years, an experience which no member of the Cabinet could or would have enjoyed.) As the
volume of criticism from overseas has grown, so the Information Office at South Africa House and its equivalents
in other countries has sought to undermine the criticism
in two ways. First it has tried to discredit the critics. They
are all either sentimentalists or agitators: missionaries who
live in a cloud-cuckoo-land or men disguised as missionaries (like Michael Scott) whose real aim is political. This
line of defence (or is it attack?) might be all right if it
were not for the South Africans, born and bred in the
country, who say precisely the same uncomfortable things.
It is one thing to shoot at Michael Scott or Canon Collins;
it is another to shoot at Alan Paton or Patrick Duncan.
Not that they don't try. But the world is not so impressed.

So they fall back on the alternative method, which is to
give the true interpretation and meaning of *apartheid* and
white supremacy to a sceptical and, alas, far too liberal
Western world. It is in an attitude of pained surprise that
South Africa defends its policies. The opening gambit is
invariably the same: "Our problems are unique. You've got
to be a white South African to understand them." As this
immediately eliminates all possibility of "just" criticism
from the rest of the world, it is quite a useful start. The next

stage is rather more subtle. "In spite of the uniqueness of our problems and the colossal burden they impose upon the white man, we are in fact facing the problems and carrying the burden more successfully than any other African country south of the Sahara." There then follows a neat statistical survey of health services, educational facilities, social amenities, and so forth, designed to prove this point and concluding with: "It will thus be evident that South Africa is the most progressive state on the sub-continent in every field."

As a general rule the pamphlet, speech, or broadcast ends with an optimistic forecast based on the general contentment of the Bantu people. Who, after all, are still only children and need a wise parental hand to guide them, a hand which is freely held out to them by a benign government (it is Dr. Verwoerd's hand, of course); and the whole is rounded off with a heartfelt appeal to the democracies of Europe to realise how firmly grounded the Afrikaner people are in democratic principle; and—with an emotional overtone which is meant to echo round the empires of the earth—"We are the bastion of white civilisation in the Southern Hemisphere. We dare not fail."

I feel it is interesting and important to test the validity of South Africa's arguments. To try at least to understand them by examining certain aspects of life which are common to all civilised peoples and to see what happens in the Union; what happens *in* the Union, rather than what the Union says for itself to the world outside. The aspects I would choose are those which most closely affect man's ordinary daily existence: the things taken for granted as normal and necessary to the continuance of society itself.

And first of all, the rule of law. And here is my example. In September 1954 Johan Snyman of Harmonie Farm,

Koster District, in the Transvaal, was brought before Mr. Justice Dowling on the Western Circuit. The charge was murder. The victim was an African convict-labourer, Elias Mpikwa. Farm prisons and farm labour are used a great deal in South Africa; they serve the purpose of combining justice with economy. And of course they please the farming community, which is a most important matter.

This particular case was to have been heard in Pretoria, beyond the range of local feeling, but the counsel for the defence, Mr. Oswald Pirow, Q.C. (a former Cabinet minister), prevailed upon the Minister of Justice, Mr. Swart, to put it back on circuit for trial by a jury of local white men. Before the trial began, three jurymen bearing English names were withdrawn from the jury. I will allow Mr. Johan Snyman to speak for himself. He said in evidence:

"Mpikwa . . . stood there just like a tree stump. I gave him a couple of blows with the hose pipe and he walked in a slow, brutal (Afrikaans: *brutaal*—almost 'cheeky') way and stood again, refusing to work. I hit him again and again. It occurred to me that this Kaffir felt nothing with his sack on (convict labourers have their clothes taken away and are dressed in sacks to prevent escape). . . . I told a native to remove it, so that I could hit him on the thighs and see if he could feel anything."

Mpikwa died as a result of this thrashing. His offence? He might have been convicted to farm labour simply for being a vagrant, for being in a town seeking work, for having no pass. But he died, beaten to death by a hose pipe.

The jury considered their verdict and found Snyman guilty of common assault, it is said by a majority of seven to two. The judge imposed the maximum sentence allowed for such a crime, a sentence of eighteen months' imprisonment.

"The jury," said Mr. Justice Dowling, "have found you guilty of common assault. . . . You are a very lucky man. If this is common assault it is the worst case I have come across. . . ."

Johan collapsed when the verdict was announced, and it is said that he wept in his cell at the "injustice" of his conviction for any crime at all.

Recently the Minister of Justice was able to assure the Nationalist Party Congress in Bloemfontein that "not a single native convicted of raping a European woman had escaped the death sentence."

I suppose it would be true to say that in England one of the bulwarks of the legal system is trial by jury. In South Africa no African will elect to be tried by jury (he will choose the alternative of a judge and assessors), because the jury must be white.

There can be no doubt that South African judges have maintained an exceedingly high standard of impartiality. I doubt if the same can be said of the magistrates. But the whole rule of law in the Union—the type of sentence imposed, the evaluation of offences—is undeniably affected by the racial situation and the racial policy of the country. Black and white are *not* equal before the law, however honest be the judge, because the law itself proclaims their inequality.

Let us consider, then, that other field of human endeavour—sport.

The white South African is obsessed by sport to an extent, I believe, unequalled anywhere else in the world. I use the word "obsessed" deliberately, for I have the feeling that Freud would have found this fact a most interesting one. Are sportsmanship and fair play always the reflection of a sound and healthy character? Or can it be, perhaps, that sometimes "the flannelled fools at the wicket or the muddied oafs at the goals" are working off some complex which must otherwise find a more sinister satisfaction and a more deadly violence? I would not know. It is just a suggestion. The fact remains that South Africa, for the size of its white population, is quite astonishingly adept at all games. It is in world class at Rugby football, cricket, and swimming, and has produced world-class performers at golf, tennis, and boxing. For a population of two and a half million, that is very remarkable. No doubt the glorious climate has something to do with it. It is almost a physical impossibility to stay indoors at any time of the year, unless you have to. The South African Sunday is a constant battle between the *Kerk* and the bowling green or the tennis court. But in spite of this great passion for athletic achievement, white South Africa restricts its sporting activities as severely as it restricts its social and political activities—to white South Africa. As a result, some very strange anomalies arise. For sport is such a universal thing —such an essentially international activity and, by definition, such a competitive one—that isolation is becoming harder and harder to maintain. Whilst in some games the African has not yet come to maturity because he has had such a late start, in boxing particularly he is producing champions: men in every way the equals and often the superiors of their white counterparts. Recently one of them, Jake Tuli (who began his career in our own school in Orlando), became an Empire champion. But he had to win his championship outside his own country. In the Transvaal, where he lived, there is a police regulation forbidding any European witnessing an African boxing match, let alone taking part in one. Recently, when Robert Cohen, the world bantamweight champion, was training in Johannesburg, he used African sparring partners (as many another boxer has done): he was visited by the police and warned to desist.

It is true that in most stadiums a section is reserved for non-European spectators. They are allowed to watch European football, and they take advantage of this rare privilege. But they tend always to support a visiting team from overseas if any international game is played. This is a little embarrassing and not always easy to explain to the visitors. It is the logical and sad effect of the policy of white domination: even in sport, even in "playing the game," there can be no forgetting, no true recreation. But it may well be that South Africa will soon find herself isolated from the sporting world as completely as it is isolated in its political thinking from the world of both East and West. Already the World Association Football body is finding South Africa an embarrassment, for there are more Africans in the Union playing soccer than Europeans. Already there are questions concerning the Olympic Games. And it is not impossible that, in cricket, other countries besides the West Indies will find it hard to accept South African teams. Just because the Union is so good at sport, such isolation would shake its self-assurance very severely. Fantastic though it may sound, it might be an extraordinarily effective blow to the racialism which has brought it into being. It might even make the English-speaking South African awake to the fact that you can't play with a straight bat if you have no opponents. It is long past the time when the doors of international athletics should be opened to Africans from the Union. If a policy of boycott against white South Africa by the rest of the world will bring that day nearer, then I hope it will speedily happen.

The spokesmen of the various Information Offices attach

great importance to "Bantu culture." They do not define
it. Nor do they tell the world where or how this culture is
disseminated: where it is appreciated and by whom. But
of culture itself, in the widest sense of the word, they wisely
say nothing at all. It would be rather hard to explain the
enlightenment of a policy which on the one hand constantly affirms itself based on "Western Christian civilisation" and on the other firmly bolts and bars the door to
such culture for the African. Nothing, I think, is more evil
or more far-reaching in its effects than this attempt to prevent the African from entering the world of beauty in
music, art, and drama. It is an affront to God Himself: a
primal blasphemy. For it is to say: "These are the most
precious gifts of civilisation: the garnered fruits of centuries of creative art. Because they are so precious we will
not share them with others. They must not be seen by one
people of Your creating, for You have mistakenly created
them black."

No African in the Union can enter a European place of
entertainment. Therefore, in effect, no African can hear
the music of Beethoven or Bach played "live," nor can
he see great actors in Shakespeare's drama, nor can he attend lectures on any cultural topic, unless those lectures
are given in his own limited university or school premises.

I have tried in the past twelve years to do everything
possible to break this culture bar: with only limited success, but with some success for all that. One afternoon six
years ago I drove to the Carlton Hotel in Johannesburg to
meet Yehudi Menuhin. As we were on our way to Sophiatown he said: "I was told that if I played my violin to an
African audience I would be breaking my contract. I
pointed out that no Africans could hear me unless I went
to them in their own townships: and that as I charged no

fee it could hardly affect the European attendance at my concerts. I was then threatened by the company with an injunction in court if I carried out my intention. I said to Mr. A., 'Okay. Take out your injunction. I will see to it that no other artist visits South Africa.'" He added with a smile, "I've heard no more about the courts."

Our lovely church in Sophiatown was packed to the doors. Old and young had come together in their hundreds from this "black spot" to listen to one of the world's greatest violinists. I am glad Yehudi played to us in the church. And I believe it must have brought joy to the Sacred Heart of Jesus. Certainly a door was opened on that dark and rain-swept afternoon: and every member of that quiet, tensely aware African audience marched through it into a new and entrancing world of sound. We formed a musical society in Sophiatown, and my friend, Joseph Trauneck, conductor of the Johannesburg Symphony Orchestra, supported and encouraged us in every way. I remember the first concert with full orchestra ever heard in Sophiatown. It took place in the open air, on our school playground, and Michael Scott introduced the performers. I think it may have been the first time that the African national anthem, "Nkosi Sikelela Afrika," had been sung to the accompaniment of a full orchestra. It was an event.

Whenever any distinguished artist was playing in the city we made an attempt to persuade him to come and play in Sophiatown. Either in the church or in our tiny little club room we heard such star performers as Elsie Hall, Michal Hambourg, Thomas Matthews, and Julius Katchen. But I think, apart from the Menuhin recital, the evening that lives in my memory is one on which the Amsterdam String Quartet came to play. The hall was packed, and in the front row there were some of our guests from Ezenzeleni, the African Blind Institution which Arthur Blaxall and his wife had founded. There was a great stillness whilst the music was in progress, a sigh of sheer joy and appreciation when each piece was over, and a great burst of applause. The quartet was obviously delighted with its audience, and the leader said to me when it was all over: "If we lived in Johannesburg we would come and play every week for your people. They really appreciate our music."

But my memory is of the crowd streaming out into the night, whilst six blind Africans went forward at the invitation of the leader of the quartet to feel the shape of the instruments they could not see and which for the first time in their lives they had actually heard. No doubt Dr. Verwoerd would have disapproved strongly. The music of Brahms does not fall within the category of Bantu culture. It is too universal, too wide in its appeal. It may even make the African believe he has an immortal soul.

Although the world is familiar with the fact that South Africa has a colour bar, it is always a great shock, I have noticed, to those intelligent and liberal visitors from Europe and the States to find how far it penetrates: how complete and absolute it is. Plenty of books have been written about the effect of Western industrialised society on the primitive African: none, so far as I know, about the effect of Africa upon Western industrialised society. Perhaps I will write one, one day. But summarised in one word it is: "Siege." The white South African doesn't realise it that way, of course. He is dead sure that he is dominant and directing the trend of events. In fact, he is walled in, enclosed, not only by his own pride of race but by this barrier of fear which grows higher every day. He lives behind this barrier as the European settlers in the White Highlands of Kenya live behind their barbed wire. And in the city of Johannesburg he is rapidly becoming claustrophobic. He doesn't know it. The barrier has immense strength: it seems impenetrable. Yet all the white man has to do is to walk through it—it is paralysis as well as claustrophobia that he suffers from. HE DARE NOT MOVE.

One day there was a meeting in the Cathedral Hall to discuss the Bantu Education Act. Africans were invited, and I took a few of the most senior boys in the school because I thought it would be good for them to hear a liberal European speaker; to realise that there were still such people.

When the meeting was over, Miss X. said, "Won't you come and have a cup of tea with me in my flat?"

I had been in South Africa long enough to react immediately with a negative. "I've got some boys with me from the school. . . . I'm afraid I must get back." (The barrier.)

"Oh! That's all right, bring them along too." (The siege is lifted.)

I wasn't surprised that Miss X. had invited the African boys to her flat, for I knew her and I knew her views on colour. But the boys themselves were astonished. The meeting meant nothing after that. To sit on the floor in a European flat with other Europeans and to drink Coca-Cola and talk quite normally—that was the wonder of the evening. It was sufficiently wonderful to keep them talking about it for weeks afterwards.

Not so long ago a high-ranking civil servant in the Gold Coast had to attend a conference somewhere in Africa. His plane for some reason or other was rerouted and landed in Johannesburg unexpectedly. He was told that he would have to spend the night in the city. He did not know that he could not get a taxi; he did not know that there was no hotel of any sort at which he could stay; he simply knew that he was at the airport, miles from the centre of the town, and that he could not stay there either. The authorities solved his problem by taking him to the Bantu Men's Social Centre and telling him to sleep on the floor. This was the first of several such incidents, and the airways were getting worried. In the end, two or three of the most famous international air lines made an arrangement with our mission that whenever non-Europeans, African or Asiatic, travelled through Johannesburg we should give them hospitality.

From our point of view the plan has worked admirably. We have had in the course of a year visitors from almost every part of the sub-continent, the Gold Coast, Nigeria, Sierra Leone, Mauritius, the French Cameroons: everywhere. But it is a strange way for the government of South Africa to show neighbourliness. It is a strange way of improving Commonwealth relations, and it is even a strange way of making propaganda about the justice and happiness to be found through *apartheid*. I don't think it impresses the Gold Coast very much, for instance; and I doubt if it impresses Nigeria. It would not improve relations with other Asian countries, either, if Mr. Nehru or Mrs. Pandit were to make the mistake of setting foot on South African soil. For they could not even go to a milk bar to drink a cup of tea. It is not, of course, that the South African government *dislikes* African and Asian countries: it is simply that these other, "less happier lands" are living in a dreamworld where it is thought that racialism is a bad thing. They will wake up one day and apologise to the white man for their mistake. But in the meanwhile they must not be allowed to forget that they are mistaken.

Sleeping on a cement floor of a second-rate club in Johannesburg is not too high a price to pay for such a lesson.

Law, sport, social life—the background to all civilised behaviour. Such is its form and shape in the Union of South Africa. But the State Information Office naturally does not feel bound to say too much about these things to the outside world. "No one can understand our problems except ourselves," so it's a waste of time anyway. But there is one even more basic aspect of life which must be considered in this context also. It is religion. I have tried to show what I believe to be the deep theological issues underlying our situation. But theology is expressed in action; in worship. It is woven into the whole fabric of a man's life. And in South Africa I think it would be fair to say that there is a greater and more general observance of religious duties by all sections of the people than in most modern countries. Church attendance is uniformly good. The Dutch Reformed Church throws the full weight of its immensely powerful influence into the scales and in favour of a strict observance of religious duties: particularly of the sanctity of the Sabbath. Ascension Day is a public holiday in South Africa. But what is the view of white South Africa on black South Africa's religion? The Rev. C. B. Brink, a predikant of the Dutch Reformed Church, who is generally regarded as a liberal-minded, moderate person, said recently: "It is true that the unity of the congregation of Christ is clearly shown at the table of the Lord. At the moment, however, a common Holy Communion of all races on a large scale in South Africa would scarcely be edifying." I think that the great majority of white Christians in the Union would echo those sentiments, though many would feel that they did not go far enough. Many would feel that not only would such an action be unedifying, it would be gravely disturbing in its implications of equality.

For not only are Christians in the "European" churches unwilling to worship in African churches. They do not believe that African Christianity can be quite the same thing as their own faith. "Look at the illegitimacy rate," they say. "Look at the belief in witch doctors." "Look at the way my 'girl' steals from me as soon as my back is turned. . . ." Not "edifying." Not respectable. Not—in fact—the same religion as ours; but quite useful, all the same, for keeping the native happy: only a bit of a nuisance, sometimes, when he's late with the morning tea or when the nursegirl insists on Thursday afternoon off to attend the Mothers' Union.

And I sit in the confessional in the Church of Christ the King. There is a little queue of penitents, each person kneeling and awaiting her turn (the men will come later on in the day). It is old Martha who is kneeling beside me now: old Martha, who used to work in the kitchen in Rosebank but who had to give it up because her arthritis got so bad. She lives now in a single room in one of the less sanitary back yards of Sophiatown, and she has to look after her blind sister. Both of them are nearer seventy than sixty. Neither has more than a few shillings a week to live on. Her old black shawl has a greenish tinge where the sun catches it. I can just see her hands on the desk of the confessional, the fingers knotted and gnarled, clasping a battered prayer book. I curse myself because I've forgotten how hard it is for her to kneel. . . . I ought to have provided a stool. So foolish of me, for she is a fortnightly penitent. . . . "I confess to God Almighty, to blessed Mary ever Virgin, to all the Saints and you my Father . . ." you, my Father . . . "I get angry with the children, very angry, because they make noise at night. . . . My heart is sore because of this . . . because the children do not behave nice. . . . Father, my heart is sore and the dear Lord is so kind and good to me. . . . He is so good to me always . . . and the Fathers and the Sisters, so good, so good. . . . And I am such a sinner. . . . So please, Father, ask the Lord to forgive me. . . ."

"SCARCELY EDIFYING." Well, perhaps our human standards differ. But whenever I hear old Martha's confession I am near to tears. I am not edified. I only want to kneel and wash those old and weary feet.

XII. Joy and Woe

Man was made for Joy and Woe
And when this we rightly know
Through the world we safely go.
WILLIAM BLAKE

I REMEMBER when I was an undergraduate at Oxford listening to a lecture on Leonardo da Vinci by Sir Kenneth Clark. It was illustrated with slides. And I think I remember that when he was speaking of the "Virgin of the Rocks" he emphasised especially Leonardo's mastery of chiaroscuro. So much of that picture is dark. But the shadows only serve to illumine the smile of Our Lady, only give a greater depth and meaning to the central figure.

I am often (well, quite often) accused of being a pessimist about South Africa: as though to be a Christian one had to see and express an optimism completely divorced from reality. But there is a whole world of difference between Christian hope and the facile, ephemeral happiness of those who dare not face the truth. Juliana of Norwich's "All shall be well, and all shall be well and all manner of thing shall be well," was based on a mystic's insight into the very nature and being of God. An insight which allowed her also to see the whole world as no larger than a hazelnut in the hollow of His hand.

If, then, I have emphasised the darkness which I see in

South Africa, the darkness which racialism always draws down upon mankind, I have done so deliberately. Not because I have no hope. But because my hope is based on an acceptance of the truth about man's inhumanity to man and about man's sinfulness and rebellion against God. South Africa has no monopoly of these things. But I am convinced that by espousing the policy of white supremacy South Africa has turned its back upon the light. It lies in shadow. I cannot help painting it that way. But no priest who is a priest can be gloomy about his job. And a gloomy priest working amongst Africans had best give up altogether. If he is not encouraged by his flock, he will never be encouraged by anything.

My recollection of Sophiatown will always be set in the context of the laughter of children: the swimming pool on a summer day, with a mass of glistening brown bodies and the noise of them splashing and the water like pea soup, so thick you cannot see the bottom. It was a good sight and a good sound to come back to when one had been walking the streets of the city or attending some dreary committee on church finance.

But I count myself blest not only in the unending joy of African friendship but in the great variety of European friendship too. I cannot believe that any priest has ever been given such rich opportunities or a life so fructified and stimulated by contrast in human relationship. It is as though the words of Our Lord had been fulfilled quite literally, as though by taking the monastic vow of chastity and so "forsaking father and mother and children and lands" one had been given all back a hundredfold. And so I do believe. I can give no other explanation, anyway, than that one given in the Gospels. It certainly has nothing to do with me. But, like the Virgin's smile in Leonardo's picture, it is more beautiful because of the darkness. In this land so torn with racial tensions and so pitifully divided by fears and prejudices, it is all the more wonderful when there are kindness and generosity to savour.

I would like to try to express something of the thrill that has often come my way in the unexpected act of sympathy or the sudden gesture of good will. And looking back over twelve years, I can see a great company of white South Africans who have supported our efforts one way and another and who have continued to do so even after association with me has become politically if not socially dangerous. For them I thank God.

One Sunday morning ten years ago I was walking across to church. It must have been July or August, the middle of the South African winter, for I remember that dust was swirling round my head and gritty sand stinging my eyes. A young European woman whom I had not met had rung up to say that she was coming to Mass that morning, and I saw her holding on to her hat as she came across to greet me. There were, as always, ten or a dozen little African children clinging round my cassock and very soon stretching sticky paws up to grasp Miss K.'s hand with an irresistible smile and . . . "Morning, Seester."

Miss K. didn't say much after the Mass except a few words about the poverty of the children. But she did say (if I remember rightly after all these years) what so many hundreds have said to me since: "But isn't there *anything* people like me can do to help? Surely there must be some way. I'm working, of course, but I could give up some of my spare time. . . ."

A few days afterwards, in the *Star*, there appeared a letter over her name, comparing the children she had seen in the Sophiatown streets with the "Belsen brats" (it was

1945) whose pictures had horrified the civilised world. It was a good letter: a simple, unexaggerated appeal to the ordinary European Johannesburger. And it was winter. And the children roaming the bomb-scarred cities of Europe were a constant reminder of the fact that war brings hunger and homelessness. Somehow or other it rang a bell, and it rang it loud. The conscience of white Johannesburg was immediately and most alarmingly stirred. Alarmingly, for the next morning I was deluged with offers of food, clothes, and money for the African children of Sophiatown. I spent my day driving our old truck round the suburbs collecting piles of groceries, stacks of old clothes and blankets, pounds of tinned food. We could not store it, for there was too much. The mail was stiff with cheques and with offers of help from all over the city. Further letters appeared in the *Star* urging a co-ordinated attack on child hunger. I called a public meeting and persuaded a well-known M.P. to take the chair. So the African Children's Feeding Scheme was born: it had been conceived in the mind of one young woman on that Sunday morning. She little knew what she was starting or how today, ten years later, the scheme is one of the best-known voluntary social services in the Union and feeds five thousand children a day. It's a story worth telling, even though it can be paralleled and bettered many times over. For it happens in South Africa, and it is, in my view at least, a proof of what might be if interracial co-operation were more widespread and more sympathetically viewed by those in power.

There is today a vast amount of child starvation in every location and township on the Reef. It is called malnutrition. That sounds better and casts no slur on society: or less than the other. "Hidden hunger," *kwashiorkor,* or whatever you like to name it, is not the exception but the rule. You see it not so much in skeletonlike little bodies (more often than not the belly is distended and the child looks fat), but you see it in the dark, crisscross pattern upon the skin of legs and arms—like the scorching of a hot fire; you see it where the hair meets the forehead and appears like a line of reddish fluff, instead of having the lively black crinkle and wave of African hair. You see it, too, in the children's wards of every hospital, in the exhausted, listless little figures which lie abed and in the too solemn, too aged eyes of a fourteen-year-old boy or girl. And if you are a priest you see it in the thousands of little graves at Croesus cemetery or the crowded burial ground at Nancefield. . . .

When we launched the African Children's Feeding Scheme we had two main objectives. The first was to relieve hunger. The second, to cash in on the newly awakened conscience of Johannesburg and to compel the government to take action. At that time Smuts was Prime Minister and the great liberal, J. H. Hofmeyr, Minister of Finance and Education. At that time (and it remains true today) every European school child in the Transvaal was entitled to a free meal at school which cost the state sixpence per head per day. African children were entitled to nothing, even if they had managed to get into school. Not through our pressure alone but perhaps with its help, Hofmeyr extended the feeding scheme to all African schools: at the rate of twopence per day per head. The strange anomaly of wealthy European children receiving a free meal at three times the value did not strike South Africa as so strange. And, anyhow, we had made a start and established a precedent. We did not intend to stop there. But we were also desperately concerned with the hundreds of thousands of children on the streets, unable to attend school, really hungry all day long.

It took some time and some experimentation and plenty of discouraging mistakes to find a suitable pattern for our scheme. In the end we established centres in almost every Johannesburg location to which any child could come every morning and for a halfpenny receive a meal worth fourpence or fivepence. Every centre was supervised and run by voluntary European workers who drove out each day to do the job, and by African assistants on the spot. Later we also adopted certain schools which had no government subsidy and could not qualify for any. So greatly did the scheme grow and so rapidly did it expand that we needed a full-time organising secretary. We had the immense good fortune to find Eleanor Ponsonby. Or, to be more truthful, I found her: she happened to be staying next door to my father's home in England when I was home on leave. I heard that she wanted a job which would involve service and initiative, so I went to see her. In an hour she had decided to come to South Africa, and in two or three months she had arrived. Ballet dancing; lieder-singing; war service on the Suez Canal and in Crete; the receiving end of the "Death Railway" in Malaya; finally with the homeless and often stateless children in Germany when the war was over; such was Eleanor Ponsonby's background (besides belonging to the famous family whose name was a household word in Victorian England). For over five years she has devoted herself and her talents, for no reward other than the supreme one of the work itself, to the hungry African children of our locations and to the study of hunger itself. And supporting her has been all through the years that small body of women who keep the centres going.

Thank God the African Children's Feeding Scheme has never become a highly centralised, heavily bureaucratised "charity." We are amateurs at social welfare, but we keep together; and, although five thousand children a day is only a fraction of those who need the food, it is at least a constant witness to the fact that there are those who care and that they are white.

Twice in the last eight years a government commission has been appointed to investigate the question of school feeding. Twice reports have been tabled in the House, urging an expansion of the existing schemes and stressing the very great need of African children and the deadly consequences of neglect. None of the recommendations of these commissions has been implemented. But almost the first act of the Nationalist government was the reduction of the twopence per head subsidy to one and one fifth pence in African schools and a regulation forbidding children over fourteen to participate in the scheme. "Native children need less food than white children," said a speaker in the House of Assembly on one occasion, "for they sleep more." I can only assume, therefore, that the children in white schools are being fed in order to save the European race from unconsciousness and torpor. It does not seem very successful so far.

With the African Children's Feeding Scheme there began for me the fascinating yet exhausting game of begging. We had (and have still) to raise a thousand pounds a month to help keep things going. But once you start begging it gets a grip on you, like alcohol or heroin. You can't stop. And you begin to look for new fields to conquer. And other people begin to look to you to help them in the game. My mail grew more and more exciting, because I never knew who would be sending me money next, or for what purpose. And strangers would suddenly appear in the office, produce chequebooks, and leave very substantial sums of money with an apologetic smile.

"Please don't thank me, Father. . . . Well, I've had a good year at business. . . . You see, I've a rule: it must be a tenth of my income, a tithe, like the Bible says. . . ."

One morning a wealthy man whose name I had heard but whom I'd never met came to the mission. As we sat and drank our tea he said: "Is there anything you specially need for your work, Father? Anything at this moment?"

"Well," I said, "I really need another school in Orlando."

He left me holding a cheque for fifteen hundred pounds, enough to build three classrooms, and a little later his brother added another thousand pounds.

Or my phone would ring: "You don't know me, Father. . . . I'm a South African of the third generation, so I suppose I've got all the usual prejudices . . . but . . . well, would you like a hundred pounds?" Or a group of European women descend upon me with a scheme for making blankets, selling them, giving me the proceeds to use as I think best.

One afternoon I was attending a meeting of our Mission Committee. I was pleading with the rather cautious businessmen who served on it to let me have five hundred pounds to build two Lady chapels on to our churches in Orlando. They were not impressed with my arguments. I said, "I will guarantee that if you vote me this money it will come back. If you give something simply to God and for His glory, it always does." Still sceptical, they reluctantly agreed. The following morning I had to go to the airport early to meet the Archbishop. I hadn't given a thought to the previous day's committee, and my mind was full of other things when I entered my office. On the desk was an old cardboard shoe box. "Secondhand clothing," was my immediate reaction. I cut the string. The box was stuffed full of bank notes, four hundred and fifty pounds altogether, and a letter to say that this was an anonymous gift. It had been left in the cathedral at the very time I was addressing my businessmen a few yards away.

And then there are the old and the poor, who week by week set apart a few shillings and send them to me anonymously: "Old Age Pensioner," written in a shaky hand on a grubby half sheet of paper, or just "Anonymous." I know mine is not a unique experience. But in South Africa today it is an exceedingly encouraging one. I suppose the cynic would say that it is an easy way of quieting an uneasy conscience, a way of escape. It may be in some cases; I would not know. But I believe that there lies behind it a deeper meaning than that: the same meaning which drove Nicodemus out into the night to visit the Galilean Prophet. A heart, perceptive of its own profound unease and emptiness; a heart seeking warmth in the bleakness of its own void. I have yet to be proved wrong.

Every morning in the *Rand Daily Mail* there is a column or two headed "Crime List." It reminds Johannesburg and the Reef that there are violence and terror in plenty in their streets. Unfortunately it also reminds the fearful and the prejudiced that a high percentage of such crime as it records is African. Few stop to ask themselves the reason. For in South Africa you soon get into the habit of thinking with your blood.

Three or four years ago a great deal was being said and written about juvenile delinquency amongst the Africans, and it was pointed out that the Africans themselves were the chief sufferers. In the ill-lit locations and in the dark alleys and side streets of places such as Alexandra Township there was plenty of opportunity for gangs or individual thugs to operate. This book has tried to indicate the more fundamental reasons for African crime. This sudden surge of indignation against the juvenile delinquent, however, seemed to me to have possibilities of exploitation in another direction. If people were so concerned about it, perhaps they might be prepared to take some positive action of a preventative kind. It was worth trying.

Our swimming bath at Sophiatown had proved itself over the years. All through the long South African summer it was packed with children from the dusty streets, free even of swim suits, abandoning themselves to the unutterable joy of cool if murky water and an hour on the sun-baked concrete surrounding the pool. But it was the only public bath for Africans in Johannesburg which was accessible to the vast population in the west. And indeed the only other bath at all was sited in a municipal compound in the city itself. Christmas was hotter than usual in 1951. It was a good psychological moment. I wrote a letter to the *Mail,* linking delinquency with the lack of recreational facilities and appealing to the European public for a swimming bath at Orlando. I have learnt from long experience that nothing is less predictable than the Johannesburg public conscience. The most needy project (such as the Newclare Squatters Relief Fund) may fail to stir it in the least. The most unlikely cause may rouse it to heights of generous response. And always there is the possibility of a loss of interest, of a new excitement to replace the old halfway through. But from the start the swimming-bath appeal rang the right bell. Money poured in from all sides in the first two or three months. I was not too ambitious at first. I felt that *anything,* even a paddling pool, would be a start. And I have always believed very strongly in the plan of doing the job first and asking permission afterwards. I did not even consult the City Council before launching the appeal, for I could foresee that if I did so I should be caught in a mass of red tape and bogged down (to strengthen the metaphor) in a sea of committees.

It took three years to raise the money. And I could never have done it without the help of three Johannesburg businessmen, one of them the director of a very large building firm in the city. They were enthusiastic. Nothing less than an Olympic Games-size bath would do! "Build first and worry afterwards" was their motto, and they did just that. We had only about half the cash we needed when the bulldozers went to work. And then, too, there were more tricky problems to overcome.

One of them was the reaction of the African Advisory Board in Orlando. I knew that I must give them the fullest and most complete confidence in the project if it was to succeed. Too often the authorities had gone ahead with plans for the "improvement" of the location and its people without consulting the Board: the representatives of the people themselves. Yet I dared not approach them until I knew that we were sure of completing the bath. So it was with some fearfulness that I attended a meeting, specially summoned, to see the plans and to hear the exposition of them. Mpanza was there. Mpanza, who had led the great squatter movement ten years before and whose Sofasonke Party had remained in control of the Advisory Board ever since. I did not know him except by repute. But I knew that what he said and the attitude he adopted would decide the future of the swimming bath. It may seem strange to those who know nothing of urban Africa to be told that any place, any group of people would lightly refuse a present of such quality and purpose. But it is not surprising to those of us who know the humiliation of that paternal, official attitude which constantly assumes the African to be incapable of responsible action. Mpanza came in and the proceedings began. It was a hot afternoon and Mpanza himself was hot and perhaps unwilling to bestir himself. I unrolled the plans.

"Here are the change-rooms: and here, you see, is a special shallow end for the little kids. . . . Yes, it's fifty metres long. . . . Olympic size . . . Filter plant . . ."

Everyone except Mpanza seemed impressed. He sat back in his chair, silent and apparently unconcerned. When everyone else had given his opinion or asked a guarded question, the chairman turned to Mpanza: "And what do *you* think . . . ?"

All attention, including my own, was focused upon that squat, silent figure. Slowly and with great deliberation he said, "Swimming baths? . . . Swimming baths? . . . We men do not need swimming baths."

I felt a wave of despair sweeping over me. How could I hope to persuade them, in face of that?

But Mpanza had not finished. "The Father is throwing sweets to the children," he said.

"Very expensive sweets," I said, hoping to relieve the tension in that stuffy room. "That bath is costing us about twenty-five thousand pounds."

"Sweets to children," he repeated. "And IF ANYONE ELSE EXCEPT FATHER threw those sweets, I would say to the children, 'Don't touch them. They're poisoned.' But if the Father throws them—why! They're all right."

It was perhaps the greatest compliment I have been paid by an African. It also meant that the bath was approved. I thanked God.

The mayor of Johannesburg, a hundred Europeans, and

two or three thousand Africans assembled on a March day for the opening ceremony. And when the speeches were all over there was a rush and a scramble. Five or six hundred children, not waiting to strip, were in the water, splashing and shouting: enjoying for the first time in their lives one of the pleasures that white Johannesburg had always taken for granted. It was a good moment.

Three days later the phone rang on my desk. "It's Andrew, Father" (the superintendent of the bath). "There's been an accident here, Father. A boy. Please come." I knew in those few seconds what it meant: the thing I had dreaded above all else. And it had happened so terribly soon. When I got there his father had already arrived, a municipal policeman, standing quietly by the still, stretched figure in the shower room. John Matlanyane. Aged twelve. Drowned. I never saw his face, though I have imagined it countless times. He was their only son, but they did not blame me or reproach me once. And when I met my African Committee a few days later: "You mustn't worry, Father. You must understand. Our people don't know how to swim yet. They have to learn, and they have to make mistakes. Look how many children are drowned each year in the dams! Please don't be sad."

Perhaps—no, surely—John and I will one day meet again. And I believe that we shall know each other, for I pray for his soul every day of my life: that little African boy I have never seen, for whom the bath was to have been a place of joy and freedom, a window opened on to a wider and more exciting world than he knew. And perhaps, after all, it was.

One afternoon at St. Peter's, school ended, the door of my office opened, and Hugh came in. That was not unusual. I have always kept open house for the children, and they drift in and out, read the magazines on my table, or just hang around for a chat. To me, incidentally, that is the logical answer to *apartheid*—just that. And when a boy or a girl feels sufficient confidence in me to use my office as their playroom, then I know that there is a relationship established which will make its mark upon their whole life. In the years that lie ahead there may be many opportunities for being completely at ease for an African boy, completely at ease, I mean, in a European house. But at least those who have been to St. Peter's will have known it, and maybe their children and their children's children will remember that even in 1955 love and friendship were possible between the two peoples: it was possible to meet and to talk on the level.

So Hugh came in. He sat on the arm of my chair and began to crack his fingers—a sure sign of some embarrassing but important request. Hugh was fourteen then, more than usually attractive, with clear and unclouded eyes, the eyes of innocence and childhood which I love. I had always found him hard to resist, so I braced myself to meet what I guessed would be a request. He took hold of my hand and wrapped his fingers round mine.

"Father . . ." he began. "Father—I—want—to—learn—the—trumpet." He paused for my reaction.

"Well, that sounds all right, son, but trumpets are pretty expensive things. You'll have to wait a bit before you can get one, I expect."

He ignored that statement entirely. "You see, I *love* music, all music. But my father won't believe in me. I want to prove I can do it."

"But why the trumpet? Why not the piano?"

"Well, I listen to the trumpet: I hear Louis Armstrong—

he's a Negro, Father. . . . Anyway, I love it. *Too much.*"

I don't remember now how I brought the conversation to a close; probably with the half-honest assurance that I would "see what I could do."

A few weeks later Hugh was ill in bed. Not very ill, really, but he lay there looking listless, and those great eyes of his had an added magic. I took my decision without telling him. On my way back from town that morning I stopped at a musical-instrument store, descended nervously to the basement, and said, "How much is a trumpet?" It seemed to surprise the salesman quite a bit.

"Well, as a matter of fact, a young man has just brought back a new trumpet because his mother couldn't stand the racket. . . . You could have it for fifteen pounds. It's worth twenty-five."

I took it. I sat on Hugh's bed and opened the case. But I watched his eyes. It was a sufficient reward.

If I had to choose a motto expressing just one truth that has served me well in South Africa I would say, "*Always* act on impulse." And after twelve years' experience I would still say the same. You will make mistakes, of course. But as Chesterton said somewhere, "the man that never made a mistake never made anything." Anyhow, Hugh got his trumpet because I acted on impulse. But it wasn't a mistake: not at all. It was the best thing of its kind I ever did. It is true that for the first three months I wondered. Nothing is more agonising to listen to than a boy learning a trumpet. I wondered, too, whether Hugh would persevere. He did. Then his friends came and asked if they could learn. I managed to get an African brass-band trumpeter to come and help. Lessons were held on a Saturday morning in the carpentry shop, and I feared complaints from the neighbours. One trumpet wasn't much use now, and I realised I had started something I could not stop. I had started, in fact, the "Huddleston Jazz Band," now worth about five hundred pounds, and including every instrument that any really good jazz band can want.

It took me two years to beg or cajole those instruments, and I have never enjoyed anything so much. It became almost an obsession with me, when I went into the city, to see what instrument I could bring back: a selfish obsession it was—just to have the joy of *their* delight, to hear the chatter and the exclamations as they handled a new and gleaming saxophone or plucked the strings of the bass. And I remembered what Yehudi Menuhin said to me that day we drove to Sophiatown: "Don't forget, Father, it was the Negro jazz bands that first breached the colour bar in the States."

The day came when the band was complete except for one instrument, and that the most expensive—a tenor saxophone. Again I acted on impulse. Mr. Spyros P. Skouras, chief of Twentieth Century-Fox, was in Johannesburg negotiating a big deal. I happened to have met him three or four years previously at a meeting of social workers in the city. I rang him up. It was always a secretary who answered the phone and always a polite excuse. This went on for three or four days, but at last I managed to reach Mr. Skouras himself.

"What do you want, Father?"

"I want a saxophone!"

"A what?"

"A tenor saxophone for my African jazz band."

"How much does it cost?"

I took the plunge. "Eighty pounds, at least."

He paused. "Well! You're a gold digger, but you can

have it!" Within an hour that saxophone was an object of worship to twelve African boys.

I have always felt sorry when I have come to read again that passage in the Old Testament about Absalom—"Now Absalom in his lifetime had taken and reared up for himself a pillar, which is in the king's dale: for he said, 'I have no son to keep my name in remembrance': and he called the pillar after his own name: as it is called unto this day, Absalom's place." I have felt sorry, for, after all, a pillar is not much use to anyone. I think I am more fortunate than Absalom, for I have a swimming bath *and* a jazz band. That is better than a tombstone.

Always, all through the twelve years I have spent in Africa, there has been something constructive to do with and for the people I have loved. The African Children's Feeding Scheme; the Orlando Swimming Bath; the New-clare Squatters; the Huddleston Jazz Band . . . Absorbing and fascinating and exciting, all of them. But I do not think they would have been enough to lift the weight of sorrow from my heart had it not been for the daily and hourly knowledge of African friendship and affection. Often enough, I confess it with deep shame, I have been impatient, angry even, at the incessant interruptions and claims upon "my" time. But God knows I would not have been without a moment of it. I have never understood or been able to understand how white South Africa can so lightly forfeit such a richness of life; can, on the contrary, build around itself such mighty and impenetrable barriers of pride and prejudice and fear. And yet I *do* understand.

There were hands stretched out to heal and to comfort men. Hands stretched out to clasp other hands in friendship. Hands stretched out in blessing and in prayer. But it did not stop men nailing those Hands to the wood of the Cross.

"Father, forgive them, for they know not what they do."

XIII. And Have Not Charity

And though I give my body to be burned, and
have not charity, it profiteth me nothing.

ST. PAUL

THE DIRECTOR of the South African Church Institute, the
Rev. C. T. Wood, in a sermon preached at Chester Cathedral in February 1955, said: "I hold that by far the most
important factor in our approach to the vital problems that
are confronting South Africa today is the theological one.
That what really matters, that what really influences the
Afrikaner, is what he thinks about God and God's purpose
for him and his race. We make the greatest possible mistake in trying to fight his convictions with political weapons. Broad cries about democracy are not the answer to
the theocracy which he has built up and which he jealously
guards—we must fight him and convict him on his own
grounds and not on arbitrary grounds of our own choosing. . . ."

I have quoted this passage from an Anglican sermon,
preached by one who knows South Africa, because it seems
to me to express a point of view and an attitude widely
representative of intelligent "ecclesiastical" opinion both
in the Union and outside it. It also seems to me to state a
truth—the primacy of theology—and to draw totally wrong
conclusions from that truth. And it assumes what I am not

227

prepared to assume—that the tragedy of the present situation in South Africa can be blamed upon one section of the white population, the Afrikaner, and upon his religion. The whole purpose of this book has been an attempt to demonstrate, out of my personal, day-to-day experience, the effect of a policy upon a people: of a policy which I believe to be basically sub-Christian and imposed by a government whose motives are clearly and unmistakably racial. But this policy could not be imposed, neither could the government which imposes it remain in power, if the majority of white South African Christians did not approve of it. The doctrine of "white supremacy" is common to both Afrikaner and "English" sections of the population. If it derives from the theological presuppositions of the Afrikaner and from the Calvinism which is their source, it derives equally from the failure of Anglicans, of Roman Catholics, and of Methodists to live by the faith which they profess. To deny this is both dishonest and absurd.

Father Wood says that we make the greatest possible mistake in trying "to fight his convictions with political weapons." This is a most interesting and significant statement, for it is almost exactly what the Archbishop of Canterbury said to me when we met for a brief few hours in Southern Rhodesia not many months ago. I was visiting our mission of St. Augustine's, Penhalonga, and the Archbishop was on his way to inaugurate the new Province of Central Africa. He arrived in the late evening, and we were to entertain him that night. As we stood in our small Community parlour after supper, waiting for our African guests to arrive for the reception, the Archbishop turned to me and said: "You are entirely wrong in the methods you are using to fight this situation. . . . The Christian must never use force . . . must never use the same weapons as his opponent." We had a fierce but wholly friendly argument, which lasted until the reception began and which continued in correspondence afterwards. I was not convinced by the Archbishop, and I am not convinced by Father Wood. For what does this statement really mean?

Afrikaner theology and English apathy have together created a situation in which men, made in the image and likeness of God, are treated as inferior because they are of a different race and colour from their rulers. The weapons used to impose a racial-discrimination policy upon the African people are, of course, political. Prejudice and fear are doubtless the motive forces behind the policy, but it is such measures as the Native Urban Areas Act, the Native Resettlement Act, the Group Areas Act, and the Bantu Education Act which translate that prejudice and that fear into hard reality. It is the propaganda put forth by the State Information Office; it is the speeches made, and reported at length, by Cabinet ministers (and often enough by opposition leaders too); it is the notices, *Slegs vir Blankes*, "Europeans only," displayed on public buildings; it is the daily police raids for passes, or for determining the racial group to which you belong, or for just reminding you that you are a kaffir. . . . It is these things which are the weapons of the white race, weapons as prominent as the revolver which hangs on every policeman's belt. They are not just "the convictions" of the Afrikaner. They are the expression of *baasskap:* of white domination. And, certainly, they are "political weapons."

I am not trying to fight the religious convictions of the Calvinist Afrikaner by any other means than the proclamation of the Catholic faith. But I do not, for that reason, believe it to be wrong or foolish or un-Christian to try to strike from the hand of white South Africa the weapons which not only hurt and wound the African every day but must also ultimately destroy civilisation on this sub-continent. I would, in fact, deny absolutely that "political weapons" are not to be used by Christians, for I believe that the Christian is bound to act politically, wherever he may be; that if the Church refuses to accept responsibility in the political sphere as well as in the strictly theological sphere, then she is guilty of betraying the very foundation of her faith: the Incarnation. It is when the Church has so abdicated her position of political trust that the state, freed from any absolute higher than itself, has assumed a totalitarian shape and a dictatorial attitude. That is a matter of history, not of opinion.

Racialism in South Africa is the same as racialism everywhere else and at every moment in the story of mankind. The ways in which it finds expression in the Johannesburg I happen to know are not far different from the ways described by Arthur Koestler and a thousand others as finding expression in Germany under Hitler, in France under Vichy, and in the occupied countries of Europe. "Broad cries about democracy" may not be a very effective weapon with which to fight this horror, I agree. But to allow democracy to lose all Christian content or to refuse to fight for democratic rights in the interests of theology— and of converting one's opponents to a more Christian theological outlook—that is to court disaster. So at least it seems to me. I believe, with Father Wood, that Calvinistic theology is largely to blame for the present tragedy in South Africa: I would wish with all my heart that a "conversion" might be achieved. But I am certainly not prepared to wait for that conversion whilst, at every level, political weapons are being used to create a condition of permanent servitude for the African in his own country.

I am reminded of the kind of opposition from "good" men (including bishops of the Established Church) which William Wilberforce had to fight continuously. I am reminded, too, of the kind of arguments used by Pétain to justify, on a religious and theological basis, his collaboration with the Nazis. Slavery would have endured a great deal longer if Wilberforce had used no political weapons; thousands of refugees from nazism, including some of the most honourable men in Europe, might be alive today if Pétain had refused to sign Article Nineteen in the Armistice Treaty which Hitler presented to him. And in South Africa, if we wait to impress Afrikaners with the truth of Catholic theology, and English-speaking South Africans with the need for religion, we might as well give up the struggle for human rights altogether. They will have vanished into the night. In any case, what are these "political weapons" which Christians should not use? In my conversation with the Archbishop of Canterbury I tried to discover. I hope I am not misrepresenting him if I say that he seemed to object to my use of "force," as being contrary to the teaching of Christ; that I had erred in appealing to the Christian conscience of people in England and America through articles in the press which urged "a spiritual boycott" of South Africa; that in using these tactics I was simply emulating those whose policies I most strongly decried. Certainly in this the Archbishop would find much support from Christians leaders in the Union. The cry has been that it is useless, if not wrong, to urge Christian action from outside, and that the only right weapon to use is that of arousing Christian opinion and the Christian conscience inside the country. But if, for twenty years and more, the Church has tried this latter policy without success, is it really so wrong to suggest a different and more powerful method of attack? That is all that I have tried to do. And the weapons I have used have been the only ones that lie at my disposal: my mind, my tongue, and my pen.

When I suggested to the Archbishop that there was one occasion at least in the Gospel when Christ Himself used force—to drive the money-changers out of the temple—he replied that this was "symbolic." Apart from the fact that there is nothing in the story to suggest symbolism and a great deal (the violent reaction of the authorities and the consequent arrest of Jesus) to suggest the opposite, the plain interpretation of that scene is that Our Lord was not averse to using a weapon in order to bring home the truth. It is at least a permitted opinion in the Catholic Church, and one supported, I believe, by the teaching of St. Thomas Aquinas himself, that when government degenerates into tyranny the subject has a right to resist. The only point in dispute is whether the government in South Africa has degenerated that far. In my opinion, with regard to the African people, it certainly has. It is for the reader of this book to decide whether I am right or wrong.

But there is a more fundamental issue, I suggest, to be decided first. That is, in brief, what is the function of the Christian Church in society? And, consequently, what is its function when confronted with a society rotten, corrupt, and blind with racial division and prejudice? More fundamentally yet, what would Christ Himself say and do, faced with such a society? How would He confront it?

An acquaintance of mine, whose judgment I greatly respect and who was High Commissioner for Canada in the Union, was with me one day on a trip through some of the slums and shanty towns of Johannesburg. I was feeling, as always, a desperate sense of frustration, and I suppose I said some pretty fierce things about the government as we drove back in his comfortable car.

He turned and said to me: "You ought to try to be more Christian about these chaps. . . . Have you forgotten the commandment? Why don't you try a bit more love towards them, a bit more patience and understanding?"

My answer was something like this: "I don't think I should find it too hard to forgive a person, or even to love him, if his actions were directed against *me*. But what right have I to be patient and forgiving when all his viciousness is directed against others? I'm not suffering unjustly; they are. I'm not segregated as if I were leprous; they are. I don't have to live in shanty town because nobody cares a damn where I live; they do. It seems to me too easy to be patient and charitable—90 per cent of white South Africa can be just that—at the expense of injustice and cruelty to someone else."

I want to suggest that there is amongst Christians an entirely defective understanding of the meaning of love, of *caritas*—the virtue upon which to a great extent all Christian behaviour rests. "Now abideth faith, hope, charity, and the greatest of these is charity," writes St. Paul. "Love your enemies, do good to them that hate you," says Our Lord Himself. And in a country in which racialism has created an atmosphere of hatred it is more than ever necessary that Christians, the Church itself, should show the meaning of such love. But does that mean that, in its dealings with the government, the Church must adopt always a peaceful and conciliatory attitude? Does it mean that I, a priest of the Church, must refrain from saying or doing anything that might wound the susceptibilities of Mr. Strijdom or Dr. Verwoerd because that would be a breach of charity? Does it mean that bishops must (as they are only too ready to do) bend over backwards in an attempt to prove that their opposition to the Bantu Education Act must not be taken to imply a criticism of anybody responsible for it? Does it mean that any attempt to arouse the conscience of Christians in other countries is proof that one has no love, no "charity" towards one's own?

Fortunately, in the Gospels there is a background situation which provides an immediate parallel with that of South Africa. There was a fierce and deep-rooted "racial" struggle there in Israel when Christ walked through the cities and villages preaching. "The Jews have no dealings with the Samaritans. . . ." An historical and a theological situation had combined to produce such a bitterness between the two sections of society that there was a real *apartheid;* an absolute division. Christ's answer to this situation was the parable of the good Samaritan.

"And who is my neighbour?" had asked the young lawyer, tempting Him. And he was forced to answer his own question. "I suppose that he who showed mercy . . ."

"Go, and do thou likewise."

There is nothing in the parable which is even a hint that the racial arrogance of the Jew is to be excused or palliated because of his background or his history. There is nothing in it either to indicate that Christ accepted the "official" excuse of the hierarchy for its attitude towards that intolerable division. The priest and the Levite in the parable who "passed by on the other side" are the representatives, for all time, of those for whom fear is a more powerful motive than love. They are respectable citizens who like to observe the conventions: but they are more—for they are the leaders of religion whose very office redoubles their responsibility and who fail in their task. The whole point and purpose of the parable is to show that charity, if it is real, must be prepared to break through convention, to shatter preconceptions, to take by force the citadels of prejudice: and that if in doing so it hurts people's feelings and outrages their sense of what is decent, what matter? Nothing could be further from the sentimental sob stuff that we so often call "love" than the exposition of that virtue in the parable of the good Samaritan. I can find no hint in it of the "don't let's be beastly" attitude which my Canadian friend was so anxious that I should adopt in my dealings with the authorities.

It is, of course, dangerous to generalise from one incident in the Gospel or from one parable; though in the case of the parable I have used it is surely justifiable to do so, for the whole purpose of it is to answer the question which this book is trying to face. But there is a wider and deeper reason why, in my opinion, Christians are so ready to excuse themselves for conniving at injustice and oppression in the name of charity. To so many, the figure of Christ is the figure of the "pale Galilean" whose meekness and gentleness are utterly incompatible with any conception of anger against social evil or individual pride. To them, all that is needed is "the art of being kind," and they think to see in Christ the fullest and clearest expression of that art. Thus, any statement which seems to show signs of any intolerance of such evils or any passage in the Gospels which has about it a denunciatory and threatening tone is hastily forgotten. But in fact there are many such passages, and to ignore them is to mutilate the Gospel itself.

Christ was not afraid to tell his disciples that in certain circumstances they should turn their backs upon a village which would not receive His teaching and shake the dust from their feet as a sign that He had rejected that village utterly. In His condemnation of the Pharisees for their distortion of the meaning of God's law and for their misleading emphasis upon legalism at the expense of love, there is no single note of gentleness: only a fierce anger. In His teaching about the final judgment, Christ does not seek to soften in any way the punishments of those who have failed in their use of this life: indeed He reserves for them the most terrible words in the whole Gospel: "Depart from me ye cursed into everlasting fire." And it is worth remembering that this condemnation is a judgment upon all who do not care for or concern themselves with the suffering of their fellow men, or rather of Christ in the persons of their fellow men. "Inasmuch as ye did it not unto one of the least of these, ye did it not unto Me." Christ wept over Jerusalem because it was "the city of peace" which did not know or attempt to understand its own destiny. But He did not excuse it. He prophesied its total destruction.

The point I am trying to make is that Christian love is so searching, so demanding, and so revolutionary in its force that it has no kind of relationship to the thing which is so often called by its name. No more than Christ of the Gospels is like that shadowy, sentimental figure so often invoked by Christians who want to live comfortably with injustice and intolerance.

Prophecy is still a function of the Church: prophecy in its true sense, that is. It always amuses me to hear discussions on the hoary old problem of religion and politics and to think what such discussions would have meant to men like Jeremiah and Amos and Isaiah and Ezekiel. For in fact half their time was spent in trying to bring home to the men of their day the fact that God was directly concerned in the way society was organised; in the way wealth was distributed; in the way men behaved to one another. In short—in politics. It is only in our post-Reformation day when religion has become individualistic that we have created this dichotomy. And thank God the tide has already turned and is running fast in the opposite direction: except in South Africa.

Prophecy is a function of the Church and must be so till the end of time, for it will always be the duty of the Church to proclaim that this world is God's world and that infringements of His law will bring their own terrible penalties. Sin is not and never can be a purely personal matter. The problem of evil affects the whole human race. The sin of racial pride, the evil of the doctrine of *apartheid,* —these are things which must be condemned by the Church and their consequences clearly and unmistakably proclaimed. That is prophecy. It is also politics. And those of us who in South Africa try to keep true to the prophetic as well as the pastoral function in our ministry must accept, and indeed expect, the misunderstanding of our friends and the obloquy of our foes.

The Church in South Africa seems to me to stand at the parting of the ways. It will not be the first time in her history that she is confronted with a choice: indeed it is a choice which from the beginning has been present, fronting both the individual and the Divine Society of which he is a member. "He that saveth his life will lose it, and he that loseth his life for my sake shall find it," said Our Lord Jesus Christ. In other words, the Christian cannot have it both ways. That massive paradox of death and life; of life through death; of the Empty Tomb and Calvary is valid not only for the individual but for the whole Church of God. To try to save some outward form of Christianity by compromising on its inward reality is to die. To accept racial discrimination within the Body of Christ, within the

Unity of the Church, is not only a contradiction of the nature of the Church but a blasphemy against the Holy Spirit of God Himself.

Yet we Christians are tempted in South Africa to do just that. In order that we may live unmolested; in order that we may be free to minister to our people; in order that somehow we may retain control of our schools, our institutions, and our buildings, we are tempted to say yes to the state and to find good reasons for doing so. That is our peril today, for life and freedom and the right to possess what we have built at such great cost is too high a price to pay for the loss of our soul. I pray God that we may yet choose death—the destruction, if need be, of all our external works; the loss, if it is a loss, of all those Christians who cannot accept the oneness of all men in Christ; the ostracism, poverty, and loneliness which could be our lot as the result of such a choice. "Marvel not if the world hate you, it hated Me before it hated you": but we marvel instead at the slightest criticism and run to justify ourselves and to make excuses.

Young Africa stands waiting, and his eyes are vigilant eyes. We have baptised him into the fellowship of Christ's Church. We have told him that he is the child of God and an inheritor of the Kingdom of Heaven. We have taught him to say "Our Father" with us. We have placed upon his lips the Body of Christ and told him that it is a pledge and a proof of our communion with one another. In every possible way we have driven home to him that truth which we recite every time we say the Creed, that we believe in the Catholic Church—the Universal Church, the Church in which all barriers of language and culture and custom are broken down.

But what do those vigilant brown eyes see as they look

at the present? What do they see as they glance wonderingly at their fellow Christians in the streets of the great city, in the streets which pass the very doors of the Church itself? Do they see any reflection of that fellowship? Any recognition of the fact that those who worship in the "European" Church desire to be considered brethren in the family of God? Any outward difference between those who regularly receive the Sacrament of Unity and those who have no belief at all?

And as they look to the future, do they see any sign that the Church is really awakening, "terrible as an army with banners," to challenge the evils of racial discrimination in South Africa with weapons more effective than words? I wonder. I wonder. I wonder.

During the past two or three years South Africa has been a centre of interest to the world for obvious reasons. As a result, many of the great newspapers of Europe and America have sent some of their ablest and most intelligent correspondents to report on the situation. Many other writers of international reputation have visited the sub-continent to form their own opinions and to give expression to them. There has been, in fact, a spate of literature about South Africa from its own and from foreign sources. Men like Charles Morgan, John Gunther, Robert St. John, and Reginald Reynolds have produced books; René MacColl, Ward Price, Cassandra, Colin Legum, and a host of others have written articles for their papers. It has been a fascinating experience to meet such people, all of whom are trained observers, and to find oneself in touch with the main stream of Western liberal culture by such contacts: a fascinating experience and also an encouraging one in times of loneliness and weariness. But all of them at some stage in the conversation have asked me the same question: "And how do you see the future of this country, Father? And what is your solution?" I have waited a hundred times for that question to be asked: I have never waited in vain. Now I must try, honestly and without prevarication, to answer it. And yet, in the answering, I am entangled in the situation itself; I write inside South Africa, after twelve years; and the span that I can look back upon is a short one, and the future is long. It is not easy, indeed it is not possible, to give a detached and objective answer. And some may say that the answer I offer is no answer at all. But here it is, for what it is worth.

In the first place, a basic difference exists between the Christian view of history and that of the secularist. But between the Christian view and that of the totalitarian—racialist—nationalist, there is an unbridgeable gulf. The government of South Africa believes that it can so plan society in the Union that white supremacy will be maintained within its borders for all time. This at least is what again and again its leaders have told the world is their conviction and their aim. Every aspect of policy is, therefore, directed to this end. What happens between this moment and the moment of achievement (1978 is for some reason Dr. Verwoerd's date for victory) is of secondary importance. If it involves the uprooting of thousands of families; if it means the separation of members of the same family; if it means the creation of inferior educational amenities; if it means a rigid and almost absolute curtailment of freedom to move or to speak publicly or to gather socially—these are incidental sufferings. For, in the kind of planned future which the doctrine of white supremacy means, the person, as a person, cannot count for much. He is subordinate always to the plan. He will be happy if he accepts it; he will suffer if he does not. His suffering is his own fault for refusing to understand the wisdom of the master race.

Now we are in the rush of this transition. *Apartheid*— the forcing of division and separation upon our mixed society—is the reality of our day. BUT IT IS A REALITY LIMITED TO THAT SMALL AREA OF THE WORLD'S SURFACE WHICH IS THE UNION OF SOUTH AFRICA. It is a reality limited to a people, the European South Africans, who in population equal about a quarter of the population of London. These men, whose boast it is that they uphold the standard of Western culture and civilisation on the dark continent and whose desire it is to lead, by their example, the peoples lying to the north of them in the same direction, are actually walking out of step with the whole world which lies around them. That they know this, no one can doubt. But in spite of their knowledge of it they are determined to go forward to their destiny.

What I am trying to say, in answering the question so often put to me, is just this. That, as a Christian, I cannot believe either in the right or in the possibility of a government (particularly when that government is a minority group in its own country) directing and planning the destiny of a whole people and enforcing a pattern of life upon them for all their future years. These things pertain not to the state but to Almighty God, who is the God of history and to Whom this world belongs. *L'homme propose. Dieu dispose* is not a platitude but a profound truth. The whole sweep of human history bears witness to it. It is because I believe it that I am so entirely confident of the ultimate future of South Africa.

The question which remains is the question of what will happen in the intervening years, and how much must we suffer from the inherent blasphemy which this racial policy expresses? Even were I not a Christian, I would take comfort and renew my hope in the obvious fact that the world itself is being driven either to a new and deep unity or to destruction. And the indications are at the moment that it is choosing the former alternative. If it chooses the latter, then the problems of South Africa will solve themselves with those of the rest of the world. But if in fact the hydrogen bomb is bringing people nearer to a recognition of the need for world government, as logically it must, then it seems to me fantastic to suppose that a policy of racial domination could be allowed to continue for very long anywhere upon earth. In other words, I believe that the direction of world affairs, the impact of those affairs upon South Africa (an impact which is already being felt in countless ways), must have its effect upon the Union's fantastic internal policies. One is driven to believe that those who frame such policies are either totally cynical, and hope that they themselves will not live long enough to be involved in their destruction, or totally fanatical in their belief that they, the white South Africans, are the chosen people of God. Neither attitude will alter the course of history by a hair's breadth.

But the question still remains: When? "How long, O Lord, how long? . . ." For in the life of a man ten years is a long time: particularly if it marks for him the period of his awakening and development from boyhood to manhood.

In a world of power, where it is possible for any government to control the weapons of power, that government starts with a tremendous advantage. And where, as in South Africa, the tradition of liberty is so tender a plant, recognised in effect only by one section of the population, the government has a greater advantage yet. And where, as in South Africa, the great forces of fear and prejudice can be linked and released as one colossal weapon of propaganda, then the government of the day, the government of the immediate and foreseeable future, is strong indeed. The weakness of a multi-racial opposition is like the weakness of a "liberal" opposition: it has inevitably a mixture of different motives and draws support from people with different basic principles.

When, therefore, a government ruthlessly uses its power and its propaganda not only to rally its own supporters but to terrify or to cajole its opponents, it is bound to meet with a large measure of success. In South Africa, the non-European opposition has been fearfully weakened by the fierce measures already taken to silence it. Most of its leaders are banned; all of its activities are open to police raids; its very existence as an opposition is made to appear as treason to the state. "The seduction of power," as Alan Paton once described it, is itself an immensely powerful thing. It is operating in South Africa on every section of the people. For South Africa is today a police state.

In view of this, the immediate future must be dark: darker, I believe, than it is at this moment of writing. There is no sign whatever that there is a weakening in the application of the *apartheid* policy: just the reverse. There is a kind of buoyant confidence in government circles that, in spite of world opinion, in spite of "liberalists," clerics, Communists, and agitators, the African people are accepting and will continue to accept the medicine handed out to them in larger and larger and more frequent doses. I would say that, superficially, there is some justification for this buoyancy. Opposition, both on the "liberal" European front and the non-European, is presently at a low ebb, the lowest that ever I remember. "The seduction of power" is

having its effect. But that this effect is temporary I am absolutely convinced.

What is the end to be? And how will it come about? I
have tried to indicate that I do not believe it to be part
of the Christian view of history to dictate the future of a
people to their Creator. Neither do I believe it to be part
of Christian prophecy to predict the circumstances of historical change. Sufficient must it be for us to proclaim that
God is not mocked and that if man persists in violating
fundamental human rights, rights based upon the nature
of man and the nature of God, he will have to take the
consequences of his persistence.

Sometimes I am asked: "Do you like (—or know—or
trust—) the African?" My answer is always, "No." I do not
like the African: but I love many Africans very dearly. I do
not know or trust the African: but I know and trust hundreds of Africans as my closest friends.

You cannot love an abstraction: neither can you trust
it; you can only know and love a person. It is the aim of
the government of South Africa to make it impossible for
a white South African to know and to love a black South
African. In my opinion the logic of present policy is to
make it a crime for any real relationship to exist between
the two races in this land; for any relationship that is
based on personality. That we have not yet reached that
situation is simply accidental. Given the occasion (let us
say a riot in a mixed area in which a European is killed),
there would be no hesitation in enforcing such a prohibi-
tion. But it is inherent in the situation *now*, and it is daily
becoming more evident. Even the lethargy of European
church people is sometimes slightly disturbed at the constant attacks now being launched against white missionaries working in locations.

In opposing the policies of the present government, therefore, I am not prepared to concede that any momentary good which might conceivably emerge from them is good. Nor am I prepared to concede that the motives which inspire such policies have any quality of goodness about them. For both the acts and the motives are inspired by a desire which is itself fundamentally evil and basically un-Christian: the desire to dominate in order to preserve a position of racial superiority and, in that process of domination, to destroy personal relationships, the foundation of love itself. That is anti-Christ.

I am back in Sophiatown. The grey smoke from a thousand braziers hangs over the streets, makes the square tower of the church appear ancient as if upon some Umbrian hill, wraps the whole place in a soft and golden evening shadow. And in those rooms and yards and playing or talking in those streets are the children whose names I know and whose characters I know too. And coming home from work are John and Elias and Michael, who first greeted me twelve years ago and who are part of my family in Christ. Tomorrow I shall take the Blessed Sacrament to old Piet, crippled and bedridden with arthritis, and afterwards we will talk about his family problems. And later in the day I shall have a cup of tea with old Ma Malunga and see if I can coax her into that deep and fascinating chuckle that I love to hear. And probably in the evening Harry will drop in to tell me how things are going at his school and what sort of Matric. results he is likely to have. . . . And my mail will certainly include at least one letter from some friend of mine beginning: "Dearest Father . . ." and ending "Your loving child . . ."

Do you think that I can give up fighting or rest contentedly in my priestly life when this is what I am trying to protect from plunder: this most precious human treasure, the opportunity of love itself? If I am mistaken, as well I may be, in the methods I have used, then I trust in the mercy of God for my forgiveness. For He, too, is a Person. And it is His Person that I have found in Africa, in the poverty of her homes, in the beauty and splendour of her children, in the patience and courtesy of her people. But above all I have found Him where every Christian should expect to find Him: in the darkness, in the fear, in the blinding weariness of Calvary.

And Calvary is but one step from the Empty Tomb.

Epilogue

WHILST I BELIEVE profoundly in the prophetic office of the Church, I do not believe at all in political prediction. Whilst I would defend in any company the right of the Church to take part in the political life of the country, I would deny as categorically its right to align itself with any one party.

Always, at the end of a conversation on racial affairs, the question is asked: "And what of the future? What is likely to happen? What do you think is the solution?"

Of the ultimate future I am in no doubt at all. It is inconceivable to me that two and a half million whites, divided amongst themselves and with no justifiable claim to *moral* leadership, can hope to mould the continent of Africa to their pattern. Over two hundred million blacks, increasingly conscious of their common past and of their exciting present, are certainly not going to accept leadership on their continent from the heirs of Paul Kruger. White South Africa will be fortunate if, fifty years from now, it is still a tolerated minority group, allowed to remain where it has been for centuries. I cannot see how a world which is so predominantly non-white and which is progressively diminishing in size (and is therefore more conscious than ever of its need for unity) can look patiently upon a handful of its citizens so determined to live in the past, so defiant of the trend of world opinion. Perhaps the

Bandung Afro-Asian Conference was the first indication of a shift in the balance of power. At least it should have been a warning to those like Mr. Strijdom, who are so anxious to maintain "white" civilisation on the sub-continent, that they have neighbours.

But of the immediate future I am in doubt. It would seem probable that any modern government, however unrepresentative of the masses it may be, can retain control of a country if it has the weapons—and the masses have not. Particularly is this true in South Africa where, if there were a revolt on the part of the Africans, the two white "blocs" would forget their differences at once and unite to defend themselves and their possessions.

Moreover, as I have tried to indicate in this book, resistance to oppression and injustice is at a very low ebb in the Union of South Africa today. There is the scent of defeatism in the air. The official opposition is, in the words of the Prime Minister, like a banana: without backbone and slightly crooked. It is also without any effective leadership. The "liberalists," as the Nationalist leaders like to call them, are perhaps stronger and more united than they have been for many a long day. But they are not united enough, and certainly they are not strong enough numerically to make any impression on the government.

The non-European people are still waiting for a leader. And that is perhaps a most crucial point. For distress and defeat can only be turned into victory—or perhaps one should say, *have* in history only been turned into victory— by the emergence of one who is great enough and wise enough to unite in a determination which had been beyond their strength. Equally, it is the dark days which tend to produce such leaders. So there is hope.

I do not think that South Africa has yet reached its

nadir. I believe that the kind of crazy nationalism which will destroy a constitution does not generally stop at destroying a constitution. And I am sure that the irrational racialism of white South Africa will not stop halfway in its *apartheid* madness.

But how the end will come, the end that is also a beginning, I would not know. I am not ashamed of being unable to prophesy such things, for I do not believe that to be the function of Christian prophecy.

It is for the Church to proclaim fearlessly, in season and out of season, the truth of the Gospel; and to recognise that that truth is revolutionary and that it is a most powerful solvent of traditional social ideas: amongst them the idea that miscegenation, the mixed marriage, is *wrong;* i.e., contrary to the law of God. One has only to place side by side the two issues, mixed marriage or injustice, and to ask which of the two is *morally* more reprehensible to see the fantastic futility of the question, "Would you like your sister to marry, etc." The way of *apartheid,* or white supremacy, is and must always be the way of injustice: for it assumes that a difference in pigmentation is a reason for exercising power. But, more than that, the way of *apartheid* is a denial of the very foundation of the Gospel itself. It is a return to the question, "Am I my brother's keeper?"; a forsaking of the question, "And who is my neighbour?" It is a denial of charity, and therefore a denial of God Himself. Nothing will persuade me otherwise. Least of all the "intelligent" rationalisation of the *apartheid* policy which so comfortingly assumes that, once black and white are divided, they will live happily together for ever after.

And I *know* the solution. I know it from experience: an experience which 99.9 per cent of my fellow South Africans have never had and would not care to have.

It lies in the simple recognition that *all* men are made in "the image and likeness of God"; that in consequence each *person* is of infinite and eternal value; that the state exists to protect the person but is in itself always of inferior value to the person.

And all these truths white South Africa implicitly or explicitly denies. Therefore, no social order *can* emerge in which the problems of South Africa have a chance of solution.

Only we, who in our ordinary daily life accept and at least try to act upon these truths, know how easy is the answer.

"If thou hadst known, even thou, at least in this thy day, the things which belong unto thy peace! But now they are hid from thine eyes."

"The things which belong unto thy peace . . ."

But South Africa, like Jerusalem, is blind.

THE FAGAN REPORT

IN THE last year of his government's term of office, General Smuts received the report of the Fagan Commission on Native Laws. Its terms of reference included "The operation of the laws in force in the Union relating to Natives in our near urban areas. . . . The operation of the Native Pass Laws, and the employment in mines and other industries of migrating labour; its economic and social effects upon the lives of the people concerned; and the future policy to be followed in regard thereto. . . ." Although Mr. Justice Fagan could say in July 1948: "One of the main objections to the . . . report is that those who have criticised it most bitterly have not read it. That means 99.9 per cent of the European population in South Africa," there can be no doubt that it had an immense significance in many different ways. It is for that reason that I refer to it here.

In the first place, the fact of the Fagan Commission is a clear indication of two things—namely, the almost unbelievably late hour at which Smuts awoke to the need for a constructive native policy himself; and the complete failure of his party and of the mass of white South Africans to accept the lead given. That the Nationalist Party had already assumed power when the commission's report became available does not really alter the fact that in any case it had come too late to be effective in moulding public opinion. It was a commission which based all its findings on three aspects of the situation in South Africa:

1. That the idea of total segregation is completely impracticable.
2. That the rural and urban movement is a natural economic phenomenon engendered by necessity—one which possibly can be regulated but cannot be reversed.
3. That the Native population in the urban areas consists not only of Native migrant workers, but also of a settled permanent Native population. (Fagan Report Digest, S.A.I.R.R. p. 7.)

Writing today, it is easy to see why such a report was not only unacceptable but was also unread. The past six years have seen a policy based on the principles of *apartheid*, at first sceptically considered and dismissed as an electioneering device; then argued and debated at every level and in every conceivable setting; finally—and the Provincial Elections of 1954 have proved this—accepted by the vast majority of white South Africans. It has been my object to try to show how this has come about, though indeed it can be stated in a very few words and summarised as follows: It is not *apartheid* which has provided the Nationalist government with its immense and growing dominance over all other European groups and parties in this country. It is not the thirst for such a negative state of affairs as "separation" *in itself* that has so stirred enthusiasm and multiplied votes. It is something much deeper and much more appealing. In a word, it is *"white supremacy, now and always."* Everything, every speech, every policy, every act implementing policy in the last resort must be measured by this yardstick. *Apartheid* itself must be secondary always to the simple issue of "white-man boss." Native laws, native housing, native socio-economic conditions, native education, even native religion—all these things (and, of course, in South Africa "Native Affairs" are always an abstract, never have any relation to living persons) must subserve this one great end.

It is not white self-preservation that is considered a sufficient motive force today; it is white *supremacy*, that and nothing less. And as these past seven years have unfolded, so ever more openly and, it must be admitted, ever more efficiently, the government has revealed its plan and its purpose.

Today the Fagan Commission Report reads like a document from another world, so contemptuously are its promises dismissed, so fantastic do its findings sound—"A settled, permanent Native population. . . ." How could such a thing be contemplated? The native is and must always be in the town to serve his European master: that is his purpose and function: that is what God created him for. If he cannot accept the position, let him return to the Reserves where he truly belongs and where he can develop along his own lines. "What are those lines?" you say. It is beside the point. The only thing that matters is that he should not, in any circumstances, feel himself part of a wider (and whiter) culture and civilisation.

So the Fagan Report, stillborn, is a symbol of South Africa's besetting sin—"Tomorrow is another day." And we who, when it was first published, regarded it as a very small step in a doubtfully liberal direction regard it now as a kind of false dawn for ever lost in the night of Nationalist arrogance and pride that has engulfed us all.